Wyclef Jean

Other books in the People in the News series:

Maya Angelou	Ashton Kutcher
Tyra Banks	Taylor Lautner
Glenn Beck	Spike Lee
David Beckham	Tobey Maguire
Beyoncé	Eli Manning
Sandra Bullock	John McCain
Fidel Castro	Stephenie Meyer
Kelly Clarkson	Barack Obama
Hillary Clinton	Michelle Obama
Stephen Colbert	Apolo Anton Ohno
Suzanne Collins	Danica Patrick
Miley Cyrus	Nancy Pelosi
Ellen Degeneres	Katy Perry
Johnny Depp	Tyler Perry
Hilary Duff	David Petraeus
Zac Efron	Queen Latifah
Eminem	Daniel Radcliffe
Brett Favre	Condoleezza Rice
Roger Federer	Rihanna
50 Cent	Alex Rodriguez
Glee Cast and Creators	Derrick Rose
Jeff Gordon	J.K. Rowling
Al Gore	Shakira
Tony Hawk	Tupac Shakur
Salma Hayek	Kelly Slater
Jennifer Hudson	Will Smith
LeBron James	Gwen Stefani
Jay-Z	Ben Stiller
Derek Jeter	Hilary Swank
Steve Jobs	Taylor Swift
Dwayne Johnson	Justin Timberlake
Angelina Jolie	Usher
Jonas Brothers	Lindsey Vonn
Elena Kagan	Denzel Washington
Alicia Keys	Serena Williams
Kim Jong Il	Oprah Winfrey
Coretta Scott King	

Wyclef Jean

By: Elizabeth Hoover

LUCENT BOOKS
A part of Gale, Cengage Learning

Detroit • New York • San Francisco • New Haven, Conn • Waterville, Maine • London

MAI 866 7216

© 2013 Gale, Cengage Learning

ALL RIGHTS RESERVED. No part of this work covered by the copyright herein may be reproduced, transmitted, stored, or used in any form or by any means graphic, electronic, or mechanical, including but not limited to photocopying, recording, scanning, digitizing, taping, Web distribution, information networks, or information storage and retrieval systems, except as permitted under Section 107 or 108 of the 1976 United States Copyright Act, without the prior written permission of the publisher.

Every effort has been made to trace the owners of copyrighted material.

LIBRARY OF CONGRESS CATALOGING-IN-PUBLICATION DATA

Hoover, Elizabeth.
 Wyclef Jean / by Elizabeth Hoover.
  p. cm. -- (People in the news)
 Includes bibliographical references and index.
 ISBN 978-1-4205-0763-8 (hardcover)
 1. Jean, Wyclef--Juvenile literature. 2. Rap musicians--United States--Biography--Juvenile literature. I. Title.
 ML3930.J43H66 2013
 782.421649092--dc23
 [B]
                                                                2012022449

Lucent Books
27500 Drake Rd
Farmington Hills MI 48331

ISBN-13: 978-1-4205-0763-8
ISBN-10: 1-4205-0763-X

Printed in the United States of America
1 2 3 4 5 6 7 16 15 14 13 12

Contents

Foreword	6
Introduction	8
Who Is Wyclef Jean?	
Chapter 1	14
A City of Diamonds, a City of Beats	
Chapter 2	25
Straight from the Booga Basement	
Chapter 3	37
Flying Solo	
Chapter 4	49
Clef, the Songwriter	
Chapter 5	61
Screaming for Haiti	
Chapter 6	73
Clef for President	
Notes	85
Important Dates	92
For More Information	96
Index	99
Picture Credits	103
About the Author	104

Foreword

Fame and celebrity are alluring. People are drawn to those who walk in fame's spotlight, whether they are known for great accomplishments or for notorious deeds. The lives of the famous pique public interest and attract attention, perhaps because their experiences seem in some ways so different from, yet in other ways so similar to, our own.

Newspapers, magazines, and television regularly capitalize on this fascination with celebrity by running profiles of famous people. For example, television programs such as *Entertainment Tonight* devote all their programming to stories about entertainment and entertainers. Magazines such as *People* fill their pages with stories of the private lives of famous people. Even newspapers, newsmagazines, and television news frequently delve into the lives of well-known personalities. Despite the number of articles and programs, few provide more than a superficial glimpse at their subjects.

Lucent's People in the News series offers young readers a deeper look into the lives of today's newsmakers, the influences that have shaped them, and the impact they have had in their fields of endeavor and on other people's lives. The subjects of the series hail from many disciplines and walks of life. They include authors, musicians, athletes, political leaders, entertainers, entrepreneurs, and others who have made a mark on modern life and who, in many cases, will continue to do so for years to come.

These biographies are more than factual chronicles. Each book emphasizes the contributions, accomplishments, or deeds that have brought fame or notoriety to the individual and shows how that person has influenced modern life. Authors portray their subjects in a realistic, unsentimental light. For example, Bill Gates—cofounder of the software giant Microsoft—has been instrumental in making personal computers the most vital tool of the modern age. Few dispute his business savvy, his perseverance, or his technical expertise, yet critics say he is ruthless in his dealings with competitors and driven more by his desire to maintain Microsoft's dominance in the computer industry than by an interest in furthering technology.

In these books, young readers will encounter inspiring stories about real people who achieved success despite enormous obstacles. Oprah Winfrey—one of the most powerful, most watched, and wealthiest women in television history—spent the first six years of her life in the care of her grandparents while her unwed mother sought work and a better life elsewhere. Her adolescence was colored by pregnancy at age fourteen, rape, and sexual abuse.

Each author documents and supports his or her work with an array of primary and secondary source quotations taken from diaries, letters, speeches, and interviews. All quotes are footnoted to show readers exactly how and where biographers derive their information and provide guidance for further research. The quotations enliven the text by giving readers eyewitness views of the life and accomplishments of each person covered in the People in the News series.

In addition, each book in the series includes photographs, annotated bibliographies, timelines, and comprehensive indexes. For both the casual reader and the student researcher, the People in the News series offers insight into the lives of today's newsmakers—people who shape the way we live, work, and play in the modern age.

Introduction

Who Is Wyclef Jean?

As a teenager in Newark, New Jersey, Wyclef Jean was known as Speedy for his ability to jet away from trouble. He and his friends had a penchant for petty crime—shoplifting, skipping school, and breaking into apartments. Once, Jean tried to hold-up a convenience store with a shotgun. (The store owner took the gun and marched Jean home.) He was trying to emulate the image of the gangsta rapper in the 1980s. He sneaked out of his house—where rap was forbidden—to listen to the latest hip-hop tracks at his uncle's house nearby and honed his skills free-style rapping.

Meanwhile, on Sundays, Jean would appear strumming a guitar and singing with his siblings in front of the congregation of his father's church. He also studied the work of jazz legends, learned to read sheet music, and mastered some fifteen instruments, including the accordion. These are but a few of the contradictions that make Wyclef Jean the multifaceted, surprising individual he is known for being today.

Jack of All Trades

All of his life, Jean knew he wanted to be a performer but refused to be limited to just one genre or style. He wanted to create his own style out of all the music—rap, jazz, blues, rock, gospel, Caribbean—he loved. The first music he loved was the drums

Jean's brand of hip-hop music has been influenced by a range of musical genres, from soul and funk to classical and country.

played in the Haitian village where he was born. He grew up poor in Haiti; so poor he often attended school barefoot. Once in America, he watched his parents struggle to stay afloat financially and keep their children safe from the gangs that roamed the projects. His father, a preacher, forbade any secular music in the house, so Jean would sneak out to listen to rap.

And yet, somehow, Jean managed, as part of the hop-hop group the Fugees, to record *The Score*, an album that broke record sales and remains a gold standard of hip-hop quality. Released in 1996, this record was heralded as the future of the genre, and the Fugees a group that would liberate hip-hop from its niche as an underground sound and make it universally appealing. It also made this barefoot boy from Haiti into a multimillionaire, jet-setting around the globe and filming videos on private beaches.

Just as he was as a child, the grown-up Jean refused to be pinned down. Jean wrote, sang, rapped, played guitar and keyboards, and produced tracks as a member of the Fugees. The group itself was a genre-bending crew that mixed soul, funk, and hip-hop. Jean refused to be defined by any one role or style. Alec Foege of *Rolling Stone* calls him "a musical jack-of-all trades."[1] After breaking with the Fugees and pursuing a solo career, he continued to refuse to limit himself. His solo work blends multiple influences, and he collaborates with musicians who work in jazz, country, classical, and even—in one instance—as professional wrestlers. Rap purists dismiss this mixing as gimmicky, but Jean shrugs it off. "I say the future of the world is eclecticism," he told Pete Lewis of *Blues and Soul*. "It's either you join us or we swallow you!"[2]

A Remade . . . and Remade . . . and Remade Man

In addition to constantly moving through musical genres, Jean keeps remaking his own image. In his 2001 international chart-topping single, "Perfect Gentleman," he celebrates partying in strip clubs, but in his 2010 presidential campaign he laid out a serious platform of reforms for Haiti. He advocates for economic equality, yet owns a Hummer with a built-in aquarium he fills with sharks on special occasions.

He began his career as a gangsta rapper at odds with his Christian father; he now sings about peace and unity while posting "Sunday sermons" on his blog. He feels comfortable morphing both his style and his substance. "When you want a fresh start, you cut off all your hair, and whatever baggage you have, you can start over,"[3] he told Kathie Klarreich of *Time* magazine by way of explaining why he had shaved his trademark dreadlocks in 2006.

Often referring to himself in the third person, he loves telling colorful stories of his exploits as a teenager breaking into houses, getting shot in the leg, and surviving epic punishments from a father who did not approve of his son's taste in music. He sometimes thinks of himself in biblical terms. After the Fugees broke up, for example, he deflected criticism that he contributed to the strife by comparing himself to the crucified Jesus.

The Prodigal Son Returns

In 2010, Jean remade himself again as a hero in Haiti. Rushing back to his native country after an earthquake devastated the island nation, he dug corpses out of the rubble and found graves for the unnamed dead. He launched a global campaign to raise funds for and awareness of Haiti's plight and spoke passionately about the need for relief on major news networks.

To the world's surprise, he announced he would run for president of Haiti, likening his return to Haiti to Moses's return to Egypt. "Hip-hop music, more than most pop genres, is something of a pulpit," remarked Tim Padgett in *Time*. "So it's little wonder that one of the form's icons, Haitian-American superstar Wyclef Jean, is the son of a Nazarene preacher — or that he likens himself, as a child of the Haitian diaspora [migration], to a modern-day Moses, destined to return and lead his people out of bondage."[4] The Haitian election board, however, did not quite see it that way, and they barred Jean from running, saying he did not meet the residency requirements.

Jean speaks about the plans for his charity, Yele Haiti, to provide relief and assistance to the people of his home country after it was hit by a devastating earthquake in January 2010.

A Fresh Start

Even with a failed presidential bid, Jean has much to be proud of. His music has not only netted him critical acclaim as a soulful musician and a savvy producer but also great wealth. He is estimated to have a personal net worth of $50 million. He is also an individual who is taken seriously by politicians and pundits. He has done a score of interviews with CNN on the condition of Haiti and serves as an ambassador of his native land. He created a foundation that raised some $9 million in the immediate aftermath of the 2010 earthquake in Haiti and is currently working on education and job-creation programs.

But Jean is not ready to rest on his laurels; instead, he is considering what his next step will be. In 2009 he said, "I feel like my career is just getting started."[5] At the time he was experimenting with scoring music and considering writing scores for movies. In 2012 he was at work on his ninth studio album, *Feel Good Music*, and insists it cannot be categorized by genre.

Jean is a rare individual who feels a connection to his past—an enduring love for and sense of responsibility to Haiti—yet is unburdened by it. He refuses to let the success of *The Score* define his sound or his challenging childhood shackle him with bitterness. Instead he uses his life story—all the many versions of it—to inspire native Haitians and poor kids in Brooklyn, New York, to strive, dream, and remake themselves for the rest of their lives.

Chapter 1

A City of Diamonds, a City of Beats

Nelust Wyclef Jean was born on October 17, 1969, in Croix des Bouquets, a small seaside town on the island of Haiti. He grew up poor, living in a one-room house with six other family members. Often his caretakers were unable to afford shoes for him, so he would often go to school barefoot, wearing handmade clothes. Jean's childhood was about more than poverty, however. He vividly remembers Haiti as a place full of magic and music.

A Childhood of Magic

Although he did not know it at the time, Jean's "parents" were actually his grandparents. His biological parents had moved to the United States to look for work, leaving him and his younger brother Sam behind. Their grandmother and aunt took over child-care duties and did their best to give the boys what they could. Despite their poverty, their grandmother managed to give each boy a penny on Sundays. They were supposed to take it to church for the collection basket, but they often detoured to the candy store.

Like many Haitians, Jean's family members were both regular churchgoers and believers in voodoo, a West Indian religion that recognizes many gods or spirits. In fact, Jean's grandfather was a voodoo priest. "My grandfather used to get these books from Egypt and study black magic,"[6] Jean remembers. Because his grandfather cast spells, Jean thought he himself had spiritual powers, too. One time, he was being bullied at school and tried to transform a pencil into a serpent to frighten his attacker. Jean pointed at the pencil and yelled, "Serpent!"[7] but it did not work. Although he could not transform the pencil, Jean retained his belief in magic.

Mermaids and Drums

Croix des Bouquets is known as "the town of the spirits" because people believe that ghosts roam its streets at night. The residents shut themselves inside their houses after dark to avoid encountering spirits. As a boy, Jean believed he had the spirit of thunder and lightning inside him. He would run outside during storms, convinced that lighting could not strike him—and it never did.

Jean wades in the ocean during a visit to Haiti in 1997. He claims to have seen a mermaid while playing in the ocean as a young boy.

A City of Diamonds, a City of Beats **15**

Spirits did not just walk the streets; they also swam in the ocean. One day, Jean was playing by the water and claims he saw a woman surface. Jean believes she was a mermaid. "When she dipped her head and swam off, I saw her tail,"[8] he remembers. Such a vision shows how much magic was a part of the culture of his village and how strongly he believed in the mystical.

As much as voodoo and magic were a part of daily life in Croix des Bouquets, so too was music. Without electricity, television, or movies, the townspeople entertained themselves by gathering and playing whatever instruments they could get their hands on. Jean remembers hearing the sounds of drums and feeling a special energy. He knew from a very young age that he wanted to make music, too. "At 2 years old, you know, I heard the sound of a drum playing in the village, and I found my own drum and just picked it up and started playing,"[9] he says.

From Haiti to the Projects

In 1979, relatives who lived in the United States came to visit. Jean was shocked to learn that the visiting couple was actually his parents. Because they had gone to America when he was so young, he had completely forgotten them. When he learned that his "new" parents had come to take him and his brother to New York City, he was excited. He had big hopes and dreams. "When I got to America, I was expecting to see money falling from the sky,"[10] he recalls. As the plane flew over New York, Jean looked down on the glittering lights of the city. He turned to his brother to tell him they were moving to a city made of diamonds.

But in the harsh light of day, the boys soon realized they were not in a diamond-studded kingdom where dollar bills fall from the sky. Instead, they were in the Marlboro housing project, a gang-infested group of high rises near Coney Island in Brooklyn. Because it was dangerous, they could no longer play outside. Instead, they were crammed into a one-room apartment, along with a younger brother and sister who were born in America.

In search of more space and trying to keep their children away from the dangers of the projects, the Jeans moved to New Jersey. Wyclef's father, Gesner Jean, took a job as the pastor of Good

Life in Haiti

Wyclef Jean lived in the Republic of Haiti for the first nine years of his life. Haiti is a small country located on the Caribbean island of Hispaniola, which it shares with the Dominican Republic. Haiti's official languages are French and Haitian Creole, a language that combines French with a number of African languages.

Toussaint L'ouverture leads a slave revolt against French troops in Haiti in 1804.

Haiti gained its independence from France in 1804 when Toussaint L'ouverture led a slave revolution against Napoléon's army. Throughout the nineteenth and twentieth centuries, civil war, conflicts with the Dominican Republic, American occupation, and a series of corrupt dictatorships made it impossible for Haiti to advance as a free nation. Few people had access to education, and most had difficulty finding steady employment. Although the manufacturing industry grew in the 1970s, the jobs it created paid very low wages. The majority of Haitians depended on agriculture to live, but were only able to grow enough to feed their families. By 1972, a stream of refugees, including Jean's parents, began to leave the country in small boats, in hopes of making it to Florida, propelled by the dream of a better life in America.

Shepherd Church of the Nazarene in the rough city of Newark. The job did not pay very much, so he also worked as a mechanic during the week. There may have been more space in New Jersey, but the family soon discovered that parts of their new home were just as rough as Brooklyn and still dominated by gangs.

A City of Diamonds, a City of Beats **17**

English Lessons

Jean could not speak English—he only knew Haitian Creole and some French—but he knew enough to tell Haitians were looked down on in his new country. He was made fun of for coming from a place his classmates thought of as backward and disease ridden. In addition to the confusing sounds of English, Jean heard something else—the pulsing rhythm of rap music coming from boom boxes on the streets and open car windows. "When I got to the U.S. . . . the first sounds I heard was a bass," Jean remembers. "I was like, 'What's that?' And my dad was like, 'Get back in the house, I don't want you listening to that music.' And of course that's the music I started listening to, and that was hip-hop."[11]

Either because his father forbade it or because it seemed to be the soundtrack of America, Jean was irresistibly drawn to hip-hop. His father's rules did not do much good; the young Jean could hear rap just by going outside. He was also able to listen more closely to pop music at his uncle's house. His mother's brother, Renold Duplesis, lived nearby and let the boy play whatever he wanted. Jean studied the lyrics of groups like the Sugar Hill Gang and Public Enemy to teach himself English and started to blend in more at school.

He also found creative ways to get around his father's rule against secular music. "As far as he was concerned, if it didn't talk about God, it was devil music,"[12] Wyclef relates. The only music his father allowed was Christian rock—music that sounded awful to the teenager's ears. But it gave him an idea: He brought home albums by rock bands like the Police, Bob Dylan, Yes, and Pink Floyd and told his father they were Christian rock. His father was not able to tell the difference, and Jean could play rock and roll to his heart's content.

A Musical Family

Jean's parents could see that their son loved music, and they recognized his talent. They wanted him to use his gifts in the service of the church and asked him to sing and play for the congregation.

Jean, second from right, attends a party after the MTV Video Music Awards with three of his siblings in 2006. They often sang together at their father's church when they were children.

Jean's four younger siblings were also natural singers, and they would all perform together. Sometimes the children were prepared, but other times they were shoved in front of the microphones with little notice. As a result, they all learned how to improvise with their voices.

Jean was also adept at learning instruments—even odd ones. When the congregation of the Good Shepherd Church could not raise enough money to buy an organ, Gesner Jean bought an accordion. Eleven-year-old Wyclef strapped the instrument to his chest and learned how to play it.

The Jeans hoped music would be enough to keep their children out of trouble and off the crime-ridden streets of Newark. Because the Jean children were not allowed to play outside, they passed the time playing music. According to Jean's younger sister Melky, "We couldn't really go outside and play, so we used to rehearse all the time. Our parents told us: Your friends are your brothers and sisters, and this piano."[13]

A City of Diamonds, a City of Beats   **19**

The Lure of the Streets

Despite his parents' strictness, Jean could not resist joining the activities of the neighborhood boys. He started to lead what he calls a "double life. Every day we'd have my dad preaching to us and we'd spend all day Sunday at his church," he explains. "In my spare time I was hanging out with the kids who were into guns and robbing and stealing."[14]

His parents hoped their eldest son would follow in his father's footsteps and become a preacher, but their hopes crumbled as the boy spent increasingly more time with his friends. By the time he was twelve, Jean had been caught shoplifting and cutting school. He even tried to join a gang. His mother bought him a guitar in the hopes that he would stay home and play rather than continue on his path of petty crime. Instead, Jean just got better at juggling his interests. He taught himself guitar and still had time to join his friends to shoplift.

Jean poses with his mother in 2005. She bought Jean a guitar when he was a boy in hopes of keeping him off the streets.

20 Wyclef Jean

Jean's friends called him Speedy, because he seemed to be able to get away from trouble and back home in seconds. But one time, when he and his cousin stole a shotgun and tried to hold up a store, Jean could not get away fast enough. He was only thirteen years old, and the store owner was unfazed by being confronted by two young boys with guns. Instead, he leaned over the counter and took their shotgun away. Then he marched them home to their parents. Gesner Jean made his son kneel on mandolines (kitchen tools with sharp blades used to cut vegetables) in the blazing sun for three hours. "[My father] was extreme in his punishments and he had a good knowledge of torture methods,"[15] Jean relates. Other incidents resulted in beatings bad enough to land him in the hospital; once he needed thirty-two stitches in his head after his father punished him.

The Turn Around

Jean seemed to be on a dangerous path that neither his father's beatings nor his mother's gift of a guitar could turn him from. At age sixteen, fed up with being poor, he picked the lock on the safe at his father's church, then hot-wired a car, set five hundred dollars from the safe on the passenger's seat, and took off. While he was speeding down the highway at 100 miles per hour (160kph), another car unexpectedly pulled in front of him. Jean slammed on the brakes and went flying into the air.

Time slowed down as the car flipped over and he watched the money blow out the window. "The one thing I could see really clearly was my dad's face looking at me, all disappointed and broken,"[16] he remembers. Though he clashed with his dad, he also admired him, and the thought of disappointing him was too much. "He came to this country and he did everything he can. He used to work in the snow—anything he can just to make sure there was food on the table for us,"[17] Jean muses. He vowed to give up crime if he survived the crash. Miraculously, he walked away with only cuts and bruises.

Rap in the Eighties

The first American music Jean heard was hip-hop, and he was immediately drawn to this genre. Hip-hop emerged from the African American community during the 1970s. Its roots are in African music, African American soul and funk, and spoken-word poetry. It is characterized by percussive beats, often sampled from other songs, and a style of vocalization that is also known as emceeing. During the 1980s, artists continued to experiment with the sound, and hip-hop diversified as rappers distinguished themselves with more complex rhythms and rhymes.

Grandmaster Flash and the Furious Five were one of the earliest popular hip-hop groups.

The Sugarhill Gang is often credited for producing the first popular hip-hop record, "Rapper's Delight," in 1979. That same year, Grandmaster Flash and the Furious Five also released their first single, "Superrappin,'" but "The Message," produced in 1982, became their most important hit. "The Message" depicted the poverty, violence, and drug culture that plagued inner cities. Many hip-hop artists, like Schooly D and Ice-T, followed suit during the mid-1980s by incorporating urban realism into their lyrics. This subgenre became known as gangsta rap. These hip-hop artists inspired Jean to freestyle, or improvise rap, both in English and in his native language of Creole about his own experiences in the inner city.

Drive to Play

Although Jean kept his vow, the clashes with his father did not end. Much to his dad's disappointment, Jean did not trade crime for the ministry. Instead, he traded it for music, and not the kind the pastor appreciated. "[My dad] said, 'If I ever hear you listenin' to this thing called crap music—crap music, I will kill you,'" Jean says. "I said, 'Dad, it's not 'crap,' it's called rap.' He said, 'Crap, rap, whatever.'"[18] But Jean knew he wanted to rap, even if his father did not approve.

Jean was passionate enough about hip-hop to risk his father's anger, but he was also driven to learn about other musical styles and master as many instruments as he could. "I remember the teacher telling me in my ear, 'You have to do more than just rap, you aren't going to make any money rapping,'" Jean says. "You have to learn how to read sheet music."[19] At Vailsburg High School in Newark, he studied jazz, learned to read and write music with proper notation, and mastered some fifteen instruments.

He also joined as many rock and hip-hop groups as time would allow, as well as performing in—and winning—school talent shows. In order to buy time at recording studios, he worked at McDonald's. Sneaking home from late-night recording sessions he would often be greeted by his father—and his father's belt. But the beatings did not stop him from pursuing his dream. He was driven by a need to find respect in his new home of New Jersey. He explains his thinking: "I need acceptance . . . so I'm going to do their music better than them."[20]

Big Dreams

While acceptance from his peers was important, Jean wanted more. He wanted to be a star. He practiced playing in front of the mirror at home, imagining he was on stage at a large concert venue such as Madison Square Garden. He also dreamed of a time when he would have enough money to travel the world. In addition to the nickname Speedy, his friends also called him Ticket, because he was often imagining himself in a far-off place.

Toward the end of high school, he teamed up with five other young rappers to form a collective called Exact Change. The group made it to the Apollo Theater talent show, a prestigious showcase of amateur talent at the Apollo Theater in Harlem, a traditionally African American neighborhood in New York City. That event has launched the careers of many famous musicians, but this was not the case for Exact Change. Jean became increasingly frustrated with his bandmates because they constantly stumbled over the lyrics he wrote.

Writing a Club Hit

Doubtful of whether Exact Change would launch him to stardom, Jean also pursued his own projects. In the late 1980s, clubs in New York City were playing electronic music with heavy, pulsing beats. Meanwhile, hip-hop acts like Public Enemy were rapping about current events, criticizing the media, and calling for political change. Jean combined these two sensibilities on a dance track called "Out of the Jungle." The song was dedicated to South African political leader Nelson Mandela, who was sentenced to life in prison in 1964 for fighting for the rights of black South Africans who had been oppressed by the white colonial government. In 1990, he was released from jail, inspiring Jean's song.

At the time, Jean had not yet graduated from high school, but he managed to sign a deal with an independent record label called Big Beat Records. The label was run by a young deejay working out of his parent's apartment. Despite the fact that it was on such a small label, Jean's track became a hit in the New York clubs. With Exact Change stumbling over his lyrics and the hit-status of his single limited to the New York clubs, Jean was hungry for more. He needed a group of musicians who could match his talent and drive as well as a big-name label that could help him realize his ambition to be a star.

Chapter 2

Straight from the Booga Basement

As the end of his high school years approached, Wyclef Jean maintained a busy schedule of performing and recording music. The status of "Out of the Jungle" as a minor club hit made him hungry for more, but he knew Exact Change could not get him where he wanted to be. Jean did not have to look far to find a more talented crew. In fact, he did not have to look at all. He joined one of the most talented hip-hop acts purely by chance.

A Fateful Encounter

One day toward the end of his senior year in high school, Jean dropped by House of Music, a recording studio in West Orange where his cousin Prakazrel "Pras" Michel was laying down tracks with Lauryn Hill and another girl from his high school. But Jean had not come for the music. "Basically, I came to check out the girls," Jean remembers. "Pras was like, 'I got two totally fine babes, man.' I was there right after church in my suit."[21]

When Jean arrived at the studio, Michel encouraged him to try rapping freestyle over one of the tracks. The producer was so impressed with Jean's performance, he asked Jean to join the group. With Exact Change still bumbling over his lyrics, Jean did not take much convincing. A few months after Jean joined, one of the girls dropped out of the group in order to go to college, leaving Hill, Michel, and Jean. The trio called themselves the "Tranzlator Crew" because they could rap in six different languages. They started penning songs that blended hip hop, Caribbean melodies, and soul, as well as showed off Jean's guitar skills and Hill's silky alto. Meanwhile, Michel was the group's unofficial number cruncher, hustling to find them paying gigs and strategizing their next move.

Ladies' Man

One thing still stood in the way of Jean and the freedom to pursue his music without distraction: graduating high school. He had failed a required math class, so he brought his guitar into

Jean and his wife, Marie Claudinette, met as teenagers and were married in 1994.

school to serenade his teacher with a song he wrote especially for her. The teacher was touched, but she still made Jean attend summer school.

Jean had plenty of reason to think the plan would work. He usually had no problems getting girls to fall for him. "I was a Mack," he later told Gavin Edwards of *Rolling Stone*. "I had spunk."[22] Out of all the young women Jean was hanging out with, one stood out for her incredible good looks: a young model named Marie Claudinette, who had dreams of becoming a fashion designer. The two of them started dating as Jean completed his math requirement and graduated. Shortly after he finished school, Jean proposed to her and the two married in 1994.

Looking for a Label

Finally done with high school, Jean was eager for the Tranzlator Crew to secure a recording contract. The group auditioned for labels right in their manager's office, throwing themselves into energetic performances in which Jean would jump on the desk, tear off his shirt, and scream into the mic. Everyone who saw them thought they were talented, but no one wanted to offer them a contract. The group was hard to pin down stylistically, and labels were reluctant to sign a band that did not fit a recognized genre, which made marketing them difficult.

Meanwhile, Jean hustled to make ends meet financially. He resumed his job at McDonald's, then switched to Burger King. He even drove a gypsy cab, or an un-licensed taxi, using his own car. His long hours rehearsing and recording made it hard for him to maintain steady employment. One night, he was working as a security guard at a clothing factory and the place was robbed. Security video revealed that Jean was asleep during the break-in, and he was fired.

Jean was able to make a little money helping other people record their music. After his uncle Renold Duplesis died, his East Orange house went to his son, Renel. The younger Duplesis bought a portable six-track recorder and created a rudimentary recording studio in the basement. Jean dubbed the place the Booga Basement and started charging friends twenty-five dollars

Straight from the Booga Basement

Lauryn Hill

While Pras Michel hustled to get the group gigs and helped manage their rise to fame, the musical heart-and-soul of the Fugees was Wyclef Jean and Lauryn Hill. Like Jean, Hill grew up in New Jersey. She was born on May 25, 1975, in South Orange. Growing up she listened to and sang along with 1960s soul records, and her parents encouraged her to pursue a career as a performer. In 1987, Michel, a schoolmate at Columbia High School, invited her to join his new music group, Tranzlator Crew, and Jean joined the group shortly thereafter.

Singer and actress Hill gained international fame as a member of the Fugees.

As the Tranzlator Crew tried to secure a recording deal, Hill tried acting. In 1991, she landed a recurring role on the soap opera *As The World Turns*. In 1993, she gained celebrity as Rita Louise Watson in *Sister Act 2: Back in the Habit*, which also starred Whoopi Goldberg. In the film, she performed "His Eye Is on the Sparrow" (with Tanya Blount) and "Joyful, Joyful," and critic Roger Ebert praised her "big joyful musical voice."[1] Hill enrolled in Columbia University in 1993 as a history major, but dropped out a year later to pursue her musical career with the Fugees. While with the Fugees, critics were wowed by Hill's singing voice. A *Village Voice* critic, Natasha Stovall, recognized her "double duty as both rapper and diva." She wrote that Hill's "smart street-smart persona and righteous, self-confident presence make her *The Score's* centrifugal force."[2]

1. Roger Ebert. Review of *Sister Act 2: Back in the Habit*. www.rogerebert.suntimes.com/apps/pbcs.dll/article?AID=/19931210/REVIEWS/312100302.
2. Natasha Stovall. *Village Voice,* March 6, 1996, p.53.

an hour to lay down their own tracks. He also recorded music with another cousin, Jerry Duplesis, who played bass.

Growing Pains

It was not until 1992 that Jean and the rest of the Tranzlator Crew would find themselves in a real recording studio. After countless auditions, a Pennsylvania-based independent label affiliated with Columbia Records called Ruffhouse Records offered them a contract. Ruffhouse had taken a chance on Cypress Hill, a Latino

From left, Jean, Hill, and Michel originally called themselves the Tranzlator Crew before changing their group's name to the Fugees.

hip-hop band, and the group had gone platinum. The label hoped the multiethnic Tranzlator Crew would enable them to repeat that success.

Because there was already a rock group called Translator, the group changed its name to the Fugees, short for *Refugees*, as a way to pay tribute to the immigrant status of Jean and Michel's family. "I consider refugees always a negative thing," Jean told *Rolling Stone*, remembering being teased as a kid for being from Haiti. "What we wanted to do [with our name] is make something positive out of it."[23]

But their label was less concerned with the group's desire to uplift refugees and more concerned with getting a return on their investment. Ruffhouse and Columbia producers pushed the Fugees to write and record songs that sounded like what was popular at the time: gangsta rap, a style of hip-hop that emphasized heavy beats and lyrics about guns and drugs. The Fugees and their label tussled over creative control, and the resulting album, *Blunted on Reality*, was more a product of what the producers thought would sell than of the Fugees' talents.

A Blunted Debut

Recorded in 1992, *Blunted on Reality* was not released until the following year because of continued bickering between the Fugees and label executives—and it was not worth the wait. The record had disappointing sales and was widely panned in America. "It's essentially the Fugees trying to earn respect . . . by trying to come across as being hardcore," complains a review on Allmusic.com. "It can't help but seem a little silly."[24]

Jean was at least able to show off his skills as a producer on one of the album's few standout tracks, "Vocab." On this track the group rapped over nothing more than an acoustic guitar. As it became clear the album would not be a hit, Jean scrambled to salvage some of the tracks by remixing them. He dropped many of the samples producers had pressured them to use, and slowed down the beats. The modest success of some of the remixes convinced the Fugees they needed to change their sound. The trio also honed their skills as live musicians, experimenting with different versions of songs to see what resonated with their audience.

Back to their Roots

Paradoxically, *Blunted on Reality*'s lack of success ended up being a good thing for the Fugees. Columbia wanted to drop the band, but Ruffhouse lobbied for them, and Columbia eventually agreed to keep them. Columbia was not eager to invest more time and energy into a band that seemed destined to fail, however, so they turned their attention to their other acts. The Fugees retreated from the high-tech recording studio at Columbia Records back into the Booga Basement.

Using the $134,000 Ruffhouse gave them as an advance for their second album, Jean transformed the Booga Basement. It grew from a six-track recorder on a table into a real studio with a mixing board, sound booth, and panels to muffle outside sounds. "It's not chic," Jean told Alec Foege of *Rolling Stone*, "but it comes out good quality, because you feel like you're at home."[25] Holed up in the Booga Basement, the group could follow their own musical instincts without being pressured by outside producers.

With Jean and Jerry Duplesis at the controls, the Fugees began experimenting with combining reggae rhythms with hip-hop songs, adding funk-inflected choruses to take advantage of Hill's voice, and mixing real instruments with sampled beats. "When we started, we were mindful of trying to incorporate all our backgrounds into the sounds," Jean said of their unique style. "Black people are a diverse group, so it's important that it all gets in. That's why our sound is different. *We're* different."[26]

Settling the Score

In 1996, the Fugees were ready to reveal to the world what they had accomplished in that basement: an hour-long album called *The Score*. Unlike their first record, this one presented the trio as rap superstars ready to remake the genre. The album was hailed

Gangsta Rap

One thing that set *The Score* apart from other hip-hop albums—including the Fugees' debut album, *Blunted on Reality*—is that it departed from the aggressive sound and style of gangsta rap. *The Score* was released in 1996, when gangsta rap was at the height of its popularity; artists like Snoop Dogg, Notorious B.I.G., and Dr. Dre dominated the top of the music charts.

Gangsta rap was a subgenre of hardcore hip-hop, a genre created in the late 1980s. Hardcore itself is a subgenre of rap that features rhymes on the harsh realities of inner city life and, according to the website All Music, "confrontation and aggression, whether in the lyrical subject matter, the hard, driving beats, the noisy sampling and production, or any combination thereof." Gangsta rap took hardcore hip-hop one step further by focusing on gang violence and crime. Some gangsta rappers depict their own gang-related experiences in their music, while others create fictional characters and stories. Many critics consider Ice-T's 1986 album *6 in the Mornin'* to be the first gangsta rap album, but Ice-T credits Philadelphia-born MC Schoolly D with inventing the genre. In 1992, Dr. Dre proved that explicit gangsta rap could be commercially successful with his album *The Chronic*, that featured sexually explicit and violent lyrics.

Quoted in AllMusic, "Hardcore Rap." www.allmusic.com/explore/style/d2918.

as "the biggest hip-hop sensation of the '90s,"[27] according to one critic. Nine months after it went on sale, *The Score* had sold 10 million copies worldwide. It spent six months on the *Billboard* Top Ten chart, an unheard of feat for a hip-hop act. *The Score* also netted two Grammys—one for Best Rap Album and one for Best R&B Vocal Performance for the cover of Roberta Flack's 1973 ballad "Killing Me Softly."

But the album was more that just popular. It was recognized by critics and music aficionados as revolutionary. It left behind

The Fugees pose with the Grammy Awards the group won for Best Rap Album and Best R&B Vocal Performance by a Duo or Group in 1997.

the repetitious, aggressive beats of gangsta rap for something more melodic and complex. The album was praised for mixing solid rhythms and skillful raps with Hill's outstanding singing and melodies from a range of musical traditions. With Hill reimagining Flack's hit and the group's covering Bob Marley's reggae classic "No Woman No Cry," the album appealed to more than just fans of hip-hop, giving them a cross-generational and cross-genre appeal.

Another thing that set them apart from other rap acts was their socially conscious lyrics. The group rhymed about Haitian pride, life in the ghetto, and contemporary political issues like welfare reform and police brutality. Writing for *Ebony* magazine, Muriel L. Whetstone called the Fugees a "welcome relief in a field dominated by rappers whose lyrics often concentrate on misogyny, violence, and drugs."[28] To the Fugees, the lyrics in gangsta rap simply did not feel authentic. "You got a lot of kids who look up to these artists, who think what they're

Straight from the Booga Basement

saying is true," Michel told Christopher John Farley of *Time*. "It's the same as with Arnold Schwarzenegger: when he jumps off buildings and shoots people up, it's just a movie at the end of the day."[29]

"Permanent 1"

Jean raps about the rise of the Fugees within the ranks of hip-hop on "Fug-Gee-La," a song that *Rolling Stone* crowned the "unofficial anthem for hip-hop's future . . . [and] an accurate prophecy of the Fugees' not-so-distant future."[30] Critics were predicting the group would be an international sensation for years to come. Jean and his bandmates tried to figure out how *The Score*, a homespun affair recorded in a family member's basement, could have gotten so big. Even their website was homemade. Hill's older brother Malaney built it himself. Fans from as far away as Korea and the Netherlands and as close as West Orange, flocked to the site to post shout-outs and words of encouragement.

"It's all a mystery," Jean told the *New York Times*. "We were trying to do [*The Score*] so that it catered to the streets. And that it did. From there, well, it just went on."[31] Somehow writing songs for and with the people they knew in New Jersey had made the Fugees appeal to the whole world. Overnight, their lifestyles underwent a dramatic change. They were constantly on the road, touring and promoting their music. Big-name acts like Aerosmith clamored for Jean's remixing skills, and he often found himself in front of a reporter's mic or camera. That meant Claudinette spent more and more time alone, wondering what her husband was up to.

Their newfound success imbued the group with the confidence to act like stars and push for creative control of all aspects of their output. The video for "Ready or Not" was filmed on a private beach in Malibu, California. Even as the budget for the video ballooned to over a million dollars, the producers conceded to Michel's insistence that the video include a scene on a submarine filmed in Universal Studios' back lot.

The Fugees Live

Even though they were becoming huge stars, the Fugees still loved and valued performing live. Their tour after the release of *Blunted on Reality* had taught them a lot about what audiences responded to and, even after *The Score*'s success, they continued to experiment with their hits on stage. For example, during a 1996 dress rehearsal for the *Late Show with David Letterman*, the Fugees were told to run through the same song three times, and they did—but three different ways. The version they performed during taping was another completely different take.

Another thing that set the Fugees apart from other rap and hip-hop groups was that they used live musicians and real instruments at their shows instead of relying on sampled beats. For live concerts, Jerry Duplesis joined the trio with his bass, along with a drummer and a deejay. Jean and his band members wanted their performances to be not only entertaining but also to cultivate an appreciation and understanding for great live music among their

The Fugees perform for an audience of seventy-five thousand Haitians at a benefit concert in Port-au-Prince in 1997.

Straight from the Booga Basement   **35**

audience members. Most concerts began with Jean onstage with just a deejay and his guitar. He would take the audience through a history of hip-hop with covers and onstage patter.

Hill remembers how audiences responded to Jean's guitar. "Even though they were feeling it, the kids were looking at us, like 'damn,' because guitar is associated with rock, and Clef is the first in a long while to take guitar back to a street audience—young kids who are not looking for anything musical."[32] Jean always relished the opportunity to show off his guitar skills. "Lift Every Voice and Sing," a song written in 1900 that served as a touchtone of the civil rights movement, was one of Jean's favorites—only he played it with his teeth. "We just do what we do from our hearts. We don't follow gimmicks," Hill explains. "If it sounds good to us, if it feels good to us, we perform it."[33]

The Fugees Give Back

From their inception, the Fugees wanted to give back to their community and use their success to help kids like themselves. The Booga Basement was not just a recording studio; it was also a place where young Haitians who just arrived in America could stay as they were trying to get established. The Fugees also created a not-for-profit summer camp called the Refugee Camp, where low-income youth from New York City and upstate New York could participate in two weeks of educational and outdoor activities. The Refugee Camp was funded in part by a corporate sponsorship of a concert called Hoodstock that featured not only the Fugees but also other big-name acts like the Wu-Tang Clan.

The Fugees also wanted to help the children of Haiti. To this end, in 1997, they staged an enormous benefit concert in Port-au-Prince, Haiti's capital city. They were greeted like heroes when they touched down in Jean's native island. Some seventy-five thousand people attended, including the country's president, René Préval. The group played their hits, but much to the audience's delight, they also performed Haitian styles of music. It seemed as if there was nothing the Fugees could not do.

Chapter 3

Flying Solo

With a multiplatinum album, international following, and a style heralded as the future of hip-hop, the Fugees were poised to dominate the musical charts as major players in the music scene. The change in lifestyle—and wealth—left Wyclef Jean reeling. "The planes went from commercial airlines to jumping on the Concorde. The bank account going ching, ching, ching every week,"[34] Jean told *People*. That kind of success fed the ego of everyone in the band, and they started to bicker, vying for creative control. In 1997, the Fugees claimed they were getting ready to return to the Booga Basement for their third album, but each member of the trio wanted to have the spotlight. As each became involved in solo projects, work on the group's third album slowed and eventually stopped.

Drifting Apart

Jean had started pursuing his own projects even while the Fugees had worked on *The Score*. In 1996, he recorded six songs in his native language and sent them to Haitian radio stations. "Certain songs just started coming out of me in Creole," he explained to Neil Strauss of the *New York Times*. "So I just recorded them, not to sell but to play to the kids. And every song I sent down here—six of them—became No. 1."[35] The songs were played exclusively in Haiti; no other Fugees fans even knew they existed.

Jean's popularity on Haitian radio partially explains the overwhelming reception the Fugees experienced when they came to Haiti for their 1997 benefit concert. Despite the jubilation of the

Jean speaks to the audience during the Fugees' 1997 benefit concert in Haiti. Michel and Hill were unhappy with the way Jean took over the show with his speech.

crowd, tension among the trio was evident onstage. Halfway through the gig, Jean took over the concert, speaking directly to the audience for nearly an hour about what they could do to help their country. Frustrated with the way Jean dominated the stage, Michel stormed off. Hill, who was five months pregnant, got tired of standing and walked off a few moments later.

A Hero to Haitians

Jean had a special relationship with Haitians and was singled out from the group for adoration by his compatriots who saw him as a symbol of national pride. In 1997, when he leaped on stage with the Fugees to accept their Grammy for Best Rap Album, he draped himself in a Haitian flag. This act made his compatriots swell with pride, something the people of Haiti—a

The Fugees display a Haitian flag at the MTV Video Music Awards in 1996. Jean in particular became a hero to Haitians both in his native country and in the United States.

Flying Solo **39**

small, poverty-stricken country mostly known for being ravaged by the AIDS epidemic—rarely felt. "When we think of the Haitian identity, it will always be before Wyclef and after Wyclef,"[36] remarks the Haitian writer Edwidge Dandicat, meaning Jean's accomplishments helped other Haitians embrace their nationality.

Jean relished his position as a symbol of national pride and was especially interested in reaching out to young Haitians and Haitian Americans. He often visited large, urban high schools like the one he attended. He fielded questions from Haitian students about being picked on or how he felt about his birthplace. He always encouraged the students to stay in school, work hard, and keep striving. "If I can help them be proud of themselves, tomorrow they're going to go to school with a different self-esteem, and it's going to help them accomplish what I accomplished,"[37] he explained to the *New York Times*.

Fugee Drama Gets Personal

In the midst of the Fugees rigorous touring schedule, Jean decided to record a full-length album of Creole music. Between his solo work and his commitments to the Fugees, Jean had little time left for his personal life. He spent less and less time at home with his wife. Suspecting something was going on between her husband and his pretty bandmate, Marie Claudinette confronted Jean with her suspicions. Jean admitted he had had an affair with Hill while they were recording *The Score*. "I was outraged," Claudinette told *People*. "I went crazy on him. I beat him up. I did everything an average normal woman would do."[38]

Claudinette moved out of their home in suburban New Jersey. Meanwhile, bitter feelings lingered between Hill and Jean, even though Hill had moved on. She was dating Rohan Marley, son of the reggae legend Bob Marley, and the couple were expecting a child. Publically, the Fugees claimed they were still a group and were working on another album, but privately, interpersonal conflicts were tearing them apart.

The Carnival

Even in the midst of the Fugees' personal drama, Jean continued work on his solo project with Jerry Duplesis; however, the modest record of Haitian music started to morph as Jean and Duplesis experimented in the studio. Jean's ambition and imagination kept pushing him to add new songs, try inventive combinations of musical styles, and invite high-profile acts to work with him. In June 1997—just one year after the release of *The Score*—he released *Wyclef Presents . . . the Carnival*.

The album featured an impressive range of musical styles, including R&B (rhythm and blues), rap, gospel, Caribbean, and even classical. Jean and his guest artists sang and rapped in English, Spanish, and Creole. "This album is such a potpourri,"[39] remarks Don Ienner, Columbia Records president. Guest artists included salsa singer Celia Cruz, soul group the Neville Brothers, and members of the New York Philharmonic Orchestra performed on the hit single "Gone Till November." The album's first commercial single was "We Trying to Stay Alive," a danceable hit that remixes a 1970s disco song and shows off Jean's abilities as a producer.

Within two months, the album had sold 1 million copies and was eventually nominated for two Grammys. The record highlighted Jean's ability to think outside of traditional musical categories and mix together styles thought to be incompatible. *Guitar Player* magazine, a publication that did not normally cover hip-hop acts, gave *The Carnival* a glowing review, noting Jean's skills as a guitarist as well as a producer. "Wyclef's strengths lie in his ability not just to deftly cop the feels of calypso, reggae and rock, but to layer those styles and tones in the studio,"[40] writes James Rotondi.

The Fugees Implode

During the making of *The Carnival*, the Fugees still maintained they were a band. Hill lent a hand with production, and both she and Michel had guest appearances on Jean's record. They publically

Tensions among band members and interest in solo projects led to the Fugees' breakup in 1997.

swore they were going to return to the studio together after they completed their solo projects. But Hill and Jean were still struggling with bad feelings after their breakup. When Hill began work on her own solo project, Jean offered to help her produce, and she turned him down.

Her 1998 *The Miseducation of Lauryn Hill* was released to universal acclaim and record-breaking sales. It was nominated for an astonishing ten Grammys. The album's success only increased the tension within the trio, and her lyrics did nothing to help the situation. On the album, she openly criticizes both Jean and Michel and sings heartbreaking songs about the pain of her breakup with Jean. According to Jean, the final blow came from Hill. Hill supposedly confronted Jean in the studio, saying, "I don't know if you still got your props," meaning she did not know whether he could still make a solid album. "That really punched me,"[41] Jean said, hitting his chest during an interview with the entertainment blog *This is 50*.

Life After the Fugees

Like Jean, Pras Michel and Lauryn Hill both pursued solo careers after *The Score*. Each had a different level of success—a fact that contributed to the Fugees' breakup. A year after *The Carnival*, both Michel and Hill released solo albums. Michel's *Ghetto Supastar* featured a title track that became an international hit single, but overall album sales were low. Although he never stopped producing music, his hip-hop career took a backseat to his pursuit of film. In 1999, he appeared in the comedy *Mystery Men*, and in 2000 he coproduced and starred in *Turn It Up*. Later film credits include *Higher Ed*, *Go for Broke*, and *The Mutant Chronicles*. In May 2007, Pras started a nonprofit organization called "prAsperity project," after his experience with homelessness while filming the documentary *Skid Row*.

Pras attends the premiere of the documentary Skid Row *in 2007.*

Of the three, Hill's solo album made the biggest splash in terms of sales and accolades. *The Miseducation of Lauryn Hill*, released in August 1998, sold 12 million copies. The Associated Press, *Entertainment Weekly*, *Spin*, and numerous other media celebrated it as one of the best albums of the decade. Hill became the first woman or hip-hop artist to receive five Grammy Awards and quickly established herself as one of the most distinguished solo R&B artists. The media's obsession with her overwhelmed Hill, and in 2000 she took a big step back from the music scene. During the following decade, she only made occasional appearances. Hill has sometimes alluded to a second studio album, but it has yet to be released.

From Fugee to Fusioneer

Jean decided to dedicate himself to his own music—without the Fugees. He made his second solo album without the help of Hill or Michel, working out of the Booga Basement as well as at the

Jean takes a break from recording his second solo album The Ecleftic: 2 Sides II a Book *at the Hit Factory in New York in 2000.*

Hit Factory, a high-tech studio in New York that he likened to the starship *Enterprise* on *Star Trek*. His 2000 album *The Ecleftic: 2 Sides II a Book* features a track called "Where Fugees At?" that places the blame for the group's breakup on Hill and Michel. He raps that he is trying to keep the group together, but the other two will not return his calls.

Ecleftic has a more straightforward hip-hop sound than *The Carnival*, but it also features what Jean calls his "crazy fusions."[42] These include a collaboration with professional wrestler Dwayne "The Rock" Johnson, a remix of "The Gambler" by country hit maker Kenny Rogers, and a cover of rock legend Pink Floyd's "Wish You Were Here." Jean describes his motivations for making the album to Christopher John Farley of *Time:* "I wanted this album to be really musical, but with an edge. . . . I wanted to bring in people from the projects and kids in the dorm. I didn't want to skip over anybody."[43]

Taking the "Crazy Fusions" Too Far?

"He's like a chameleon," explains his sister, Melky Jean, who also sings backup on his records. "He can adapt from rap to pop to country because, growing up, that's what he used to listen to; he never limited himself."[44] Jean is always singing or rapping to himself. For example, he'll hum a classic rock song that he then improvises into a reggae-inflected hook. His musical restlessness shows on *Ecleftic*, which features an irreverent anthem to strip clubs, a soulful love tune, and a song memorializing Amadou Diallo, a young African immigrant shot to death by police officers in New York.

This sampling of musical styles paid off on *Ecleftic*, which Farley describes as a "a pop-music search engine, filtering through genres, highlighting what's melodious and spirited."[45] Though its sales did not compare to those of *The Carnival, Ecleftic* climbed to a respectable number nine on the *Billboard* 200.

But by 2002, with the release of his next album, *Masquerade*, critics were getting tired of what they saw as Jean's gimmick of

Flying Solo

Pink Floyd

As a teenager, Jean counted British rockers Pink Floyd as one of his favorite bands and was able to listen to them because his father thought they were Christian rock. Jean paid tribute to them on his 2000 album *The Ecleftic* with a cover of their "Wish You Were Here."

While it was unusual for rappers to flaunt their love of rock, Jean admired the guitar skills of Syd Barrett, who founded Pink Floyd in 1965. Barrett was deeply influenced by rhythm and blues and jazz. He named the group by combining the first names of two blues musicians, Pink Anderson and Floyd Council. David Gilmour, who filled Barrett's role after he left, is also well known for his slow, bluesy style on the electric guitar.

As a psychedelic and progressive rock band, Pink Floyd's music was experimental. They tried to sonically reproduce the experience of mind-altering psychedelic drugs and also aimed to raise rock music to greater artistic levels. Their most popular albums are *The Dark Side of the Moon* (1973), *Wish You Were Here* (1975), and *The Wall* (1979). They wrote concept albums that were each united by an overall theme or narrative. *Wish You Were Here*, for example, is about the absence of Barrett, who left after suffering a nervous breakdown, and the effect this had on the band.

---

mixing incongruous musical styles. "Yet another overreaching, overlong musical erector set," complained Nathan Rabin on the *A.V. Club* blog about Jean's third solo record. "The album offers an uneven, conceptually muddled tour of the rapper's current musical obsessions, from gritty underground hip-hop to Caribbean music,"[46] Rabin writes. Sal Cinquemani of *Slant Magazine* called it "yet another concept album," before adding that the rock tracks "fall flat."[47]

Reconciliations

While critics were wondering whether Jean was in a stylistic rut, his personal relationships were evolving—for the better. Jean and Claudinette reconciled shortly after she stormed out of the house and were working to make their relationship stronger. "They've been through tough times, but they're still together," says R&B and gospel singer Patti LaBelle, who has collaborated with Jean and knows the couple well. "It's a wonderful relationship."[48]

Jean also wanted to set aside differences with his former Fugees band members. He reached out to both Michel and Hill, but only Michel called back. "Pras is like a little brother to me," Jean explains. "As men . . . you're going to have differences."[49] But the two of them were able to put those differences aside and begin rebuilding their friendship.

Moving On, Moving Out

In 2000, Jean decided he needed to move out of the Booga Basement and into a better studio. He and Duplesis took their time selecting the new space, a full-sized recording studio in midtown Manhattan they called Platinum Sound. Jean decided to commission an artist to paint a mural on the studio's wall and instructed the artist to include a painting of his father's church. "This is where it all began,"[50] he remarks, while showing off the mural on a video interview.

Even as he paid tribute to them on his studio wall, Jean's relationship with his parents remained complicated. Although Jean's career meant stardom, money, and accolades, his mother was unimpressed. She thought he was wasting his singing voice on rap tracks. "My mom, she's not impressed with any of the rap stuff that I do," says Jean. "She's always, like, 'What songs are you singing?'"[51] Jean's mother worries that her son is letting his voice—trained to sing hymns in church—go to waste.

Meanwhile, the fact that *Ecleftic* contained a song celebrating topless bars and a skit about Jean visiting strip clubs while on

Flying Solo

tour did not help relations with his dad. The preacher was not impressed either by the wealth that the "devil's music" provided to his son; however, the two began to reconcile as the elder Jean found a way to do the Lord's work with what the devil's music provided. During his visits to his son's home, he raided the hip-hop star's closet, carting off shoes and clothes to give to the poor. "My dad would come to my house and he'd be like, 'You have more sneakers than Will Smith!'" Jean tells *People*. "He'd raid my closet and half my [Nike] Jordans would be gone, my [Giorgio] Armani suits. He'd just bag 'em and go give 'em away."[52]

Still a Preacher's Son

Although his parents were disapproving of their son's lifestyle, Jean felt a deep affection for both his parents. "My father took care of us since we were little," Jean tells Gavin Edwards of *Rolling Stone*. "It's only right that I take care of my parents now."[53] Jean made sure to spend as much time as possible with his aging parents. In the summer of 2000, Jean's father went missing for a few days—presumably wandering off because of dementia, a deterioration of brain function common in elderly adults. He was found in a hospital, much to his son's relief.

As his relationships with his wife, parents, and old friends deepened, Jean's music was also ready to mature. With a brand new studio and his longtime producing partner, Jerry Duplesis, it was time for Jean to explore his more soulful side and reconnect with his songwriting gifts.

Chapter 4

Clef, the Songwriter

With *The Carnival* and *Ecleftic*, Wyclef Jean had established himself as a solo artist with a distinctive style. He was known as the hip-hop artist who could bring together diverse musical genres on a single track. His albums showed his talent as a producer, layering seemingly incongruous styles into a cohesive whole. But Jean wanted to be known for more than his production skills and danceable hits. He wanted to be taken seriously as a songwriter. A horrible tragedy would eventually find its way into Jean's song lyrics, bringing him success born of pain.

Tragedy Strikes

Even as Jean and his father grew closer, Gesner Jean refused to attend his son's concerts, still maintaining that Jean wrote music that was counter to Christian teachings. The elder Jean knew almost nothing about his son's stardom. Samuel Jean, Wyclef Jean's younger brother, remembers that during one of his father's visits to Manhattan Wyclef was mobbed by fans on the street. This left his father shocked and baffled.

In January 2001, Jean hosted a benefit concert at Carnegie Hall to raise money for a nonprofit organization that served low-income children. Because the event was for a good cause, the elder Jean relented on his boycott of his son's performances. When his son appeared on stage in a white tuxedo, Gesner Jean smiled. According to Samuel Jean, after the concert the two grew even closer and were learning to live with their differences. "[My father] had accepted the fact that 'My son makes the kind of music that I don't like,'"[54] Samuel told Stephen Kurczy of the *Christian Science Monitor.*

Jean did not get to enjoy his father's newfound acceptance for long. In September 2001, Gesner Jean was killed in a freak accident. Details remain sketchy, but the elder Jean was either crushed by a car he was repairing or pinned against the garage door by his son's Bentley. The police investigated the incident but found no evidence of foul play. Jean was in the studio at the time of the accident, and he rushed to the hospital, but by the time he got there his father was dead. Gesner Jean was only sixty years old.

Jean was devastated by his father's death and poured his energies and considerable financial resources into a lavish funeral. Gesner Jean, a Haitian immigrant who spent most of his life struggling to make ends meet, was buried in a gold coffin carried by horses. "I gave him a very royal funeral, because to me my Dad was a king," Jean told Julia Llewellyn Smith of the London *Daily Telegraph.* "I'd have spent all my millions, sold all my cars and houses to give him that funeral."[55]

Memorializing His Dad in Song

The year 2001 continued to be a difficult one for the Jeans. After Jean's father died, both his mother-in-law and his wife's uncle passed away. The couple entered a dark period of mourning. Then after a year, Jean decided he wanted to memorialize his father, not with a lavish funeral, but in song. "I finally understood: To conquer death, you have to celebrate life,"[56] Jean said. To do that, he returned to the studio to work on an album with a distinctly different sound from his previous music.

On the 2003 album *The Preacher's Son* Jean returns to his roots as a singer and songwriter. Like his previous albums, *The Preacher's Son* features collaborations with high-profile acts such as rap star Missy Elliot, Latino guitar sensation Carlos Santana, and R&B icon Patti LaBelle. On this record, however, he leaves the rapping to his guest stars and instead sings on stripped-down tracks. Rather than feature Jean's ability as a producer to mix eclectic beats and samples, this album focuses on Jean's talents as a songwriter.

Wyclef Jean, Actor

In addition to his musical career, Jean has also appeared in several films and television shows, starting with MTV's 2001 musical film *Carmen: A Hip Hopera*, in which he played a fortune-teller. He also appeared in Cess Silvera's *Shottas*, a Jamaican gangster movie, which was released in 2002 in Jamaica and in 2006 in the United States.

Jean performs on an episode of Third Watch *in 2005.*

In 2005, Jean appeared on NBC's hit series *Third Watch*, a drama about New York City police officers, firefighters, and paramedics who worked the 3:00-to-11:00-P.M. shift in the same precinct. Jean played the character of Marcel Hollis, a Jamaican-born drug dealer who orchestrates the bombing of the police precinct house at the end of the final season. Jean acted in another crime drama that same year, Chris Fisher's film *Dirty*. He was again cast as a leading gangster named Damian Baine, who sends two undercover police officers—who are also former gang members—to bust a dangerous rival gang.

Although his acting career has barely exceeded these titles, he has written, produced, and contributed to numerous film and television soundtracks, including *Shottas*, *Love Actually*, *50 First Dates*, *Dirty Dancing: Havana Nights*, and the hit HBO series *Entourage*.

A New Label for a New Style

The shift in tone on *The Preacher's Son* can be attributed to Jean's personal experiences in 2001, but it also had to do with a change in studios. Although Columbia had helped Jean sell some 3 million records, he wanted a studio that would allow him to focus his creative energies on songs that were distinctive and not necessarily based on what was popular. He struck a deal with producer and music executive Clive Davis, who had recently created his own label called J Records.

Jean had worked with Davis before. The two had teamed up to write and produce "Maria, Maria," a single performed by Santana that spent ten weeks at number one on *Billboard*'s Hot 100. They also collaborated on Whitney Houston's single "My Love Is Your

Jean and Clive Davis appear at a listening party for The Preacher's Son in 2003.

Love," which sold 3 million copies worldwide. When Davis left a larger company to start his own label, Jean was happy to join his former collaborator.

According to Davis it was a "no-brainer" to work with Jean, and Jean was eager to team up with someone who would afford him greater artistic freedom. "Whenever I get with Clive, he has me focused on my songwriting ability," Jean reports. "There were no mixed messages from him. It was just 'Do what you do best—music.'"[57]

A New Version of Success

Critics embraced Jean's new sound. Allmusic.com reviewer Rob Theakston called *The Preacher's Son* a "redemption" from the lackluster *Masquerade*. According to Theakston, "[The album] finds Wyclef re-energized right from the opening moments.... *The Preacher's Son* is a welcome return to form and easily one of the biggest highlights of Wyclef's career."[58] In *Billboard* Michael Paoletta asserted, "'The Preacher's Son' proves that Jean is in a class of his own."[59]

Though the critics loved it, the album had only modest sales. It climbed to number five on the R&B charts, but only made it to number twenty-two on the *Billboard* 200. However, Jean viewed the album as a success because it remained true to his artistic vision and did not bend to popular tastes. "I'm not the kind of cat that finds out what beats are rocking in the clubs and then finds their producers [to make those beats for me] to put my voice over," he explains to Rashaun Hall of *Billboard*. "I don't want to have to adjust to that sound. I have the Clef sound. It's a very rebel sound."[60]

In his early thirties and having experienced the death of three people close to him, Jean was thinking about how he was going to be remembered. "These songs [on *Preacher's Son*] are going to be my legacy,"[61] he told Ernie Rideout in *Keyboard*. He was proud of his new songs and could barely contain his eagerness to perform them. "I feel it, the vibe and the energy," he told *People*. "Get ready for the shows, man. It's going to be off the hook."[62]

A Fugees Reunion

In 2004, comedian Dave Chappelle staged a concert in Bedford-Stuyvesant, Brooklyn, for his documentary film *Block Party*. The Fugees reunited for the show, and performed along with other hip-hop, rap, and neo-soul artists, including The Roots, Erykah Badu, Mos Def, and Kanye West. The Fugees' set consisted of "Nappy Heads," one of the few hits on *Blunted on Reality*, followed by Hill's well-received solo rendition of "Killing Me Softly with His Song." Jean then performed an early version of "[If I Was] President" with the Central State University Marching Band.

The Fugees appeared together for a second time the following summer, when they opened for Black Entertainment Television's 2005 music awards. The group announced plans for a new album and released a single called "Take It Easy" that September. Then, for the first time since 1997, they went on tour in Europe. Yet neither the single nor the tour generated the same public excitement as their earlier music, and the Fugees could not escape past differences to push the album forward. It was postponed with no promise of release as the group parted ways for a second time in 2006. Looking back, Jean remarks that "those Fugees reunion shows shouldn't have been done, because we wasn't ready."

Quoted in Pete Lewis. "Wyclef Jean: Perfect Gentleman." *Blues & Soul*, December 2008. www.bluesandsoul.com/feature/360/wyclef_jean_perfect_gentleman.

Songs for Peace and Unity

Whereas *The Carnival* and *Ecleftic* included party anthems celebrating strippers and drinking, *The Preacher's Son* was more introspective and featured a number of songs that focused on social and political issues. An interest in music about social and political change became a defining feature of Jean's music from then on. For example, in 2004, Jean wrote the song "A Million Voices" for the film *Hotel Rwanda*, a movie based on the true story of a hotel manager in Rwanda who sheltered over a thousand refugees fleeing ethnic violence. In his song, Jean calls on the nations of Africa to unite and set aside ethnic differences. The song was nominated for both a Golden Globe and a Grammy Award.

Jean expresses these wishes in mediums other than songs. In a February 19, 2005, *Billboard* editorial, for example, Jean writes about the failure of the international community to stop the violence in Rwanda. Readers familiar with Jean's bouncy dance hits

Jean attends the 2004 premiere of Hotel Rwanda, for which he wrote the song "A Million Voices."

may have been surprised to read his thoughtful history of the political changes that led up to the country's civil war. But Jean was clear and forceful in his call to action. "We can make an impact on world issues," he declares. "Let us not ignore part of the world, for we are part of the whole world. Teach those who can't read to read, bring medicine to those who are sick, give food to those who are hungry."[63] In this editorial, Jean starts to sound a little like his father.

The United Nations on an Album

Jean continued to treat social and political themes in his 2007 album *The Carnival II: Memoirs of an Immigrant*. He wanted the title to reference his first studio album, because they are both, according to him, "multicultural albums"[64] that feature duets with performers from various genres and songs that mix incongruous musical styles. He teamed up with vocalist Norah Jones for a soulful duet about Hurricane Katrina and sang with pop legend Paul Simon about Sean Bell, an unarmed African American man shot by New York City police officers right before his wedding.

The overall theme of the album is the experience of immigrants, but Jean was also thinking about how music can unify people from different cultures. "There's a revolution of culture going on around the world where The United Nations is everywhere," Jean told Pete Lewis of *Blues & Soul*. "You go into a room, and everybody's from a different country. It's like we're *all* immigrants."[65] *The Carnival II* was meant to be a musical United Nations.

The critical reception of *The Carnival II* was a mixed bag. On RapReviews.com, Steve Juon remarks that Jean is "one of rap's best kept secrets" and declares "the time has long since come to recognize [that Jean's] music skills are up to par with any big name hip-hop hit maker" and that Jean has made "some of the best hip-hop music out there, simply because he refuses to limit himself to one style."[66] In contrast, Kelefa Sanneh, of the *New York Times* complains that the album is "yet another mishmash, this one a cosmopolitan hip-hop grab bag full of big-name guests, baffling miscalculations and bursts of inspired songwriting."[67]

Jean performs in 2007 with Norah Jones, who appeared on his album The Carnival II: Memoirs of an Immigrant.

Starting a Family

Jean remained unconcerned about the critics' complaints. He was busy making music—not only his own but also producing for other artists—and was thinking of starting a family. In 2001, Claudinette created Fusha Designs, a fashion company to produce her luxurious clothing line. As her husband's career took off, so did her own. By the time *The Preacher's Son* was released, she was already established as a designer for high-profile acts such as Mary J. Blige, Whitney Houston, and, of course, Jean. When Jean and his band wore Fusha at the European MTV Awards, Jean was named one of the ten best-dressed men by *In Style* magazine.

With both of their careers firmly established, the couple decided it was time to have children. In 2005, Jean and his wife adopted a three-day-old Guianan-Haitian orphan. They named her Angelina Claudinette Jean. Although the Jeans were close friends with Angelina Jolie, they told reporters the girl was not named after the actress. Rather they picked her name because she seemed like an angel to them.

Jean and wife Marie Claudinette walk the runway at a show for her fashion line, Fusha Designs, in 2005.

In 2009, Marie Claudinette and Jean celebrated their fifteenth wedding anniversary by renewing their vows. The couple held a ceremony for family and friends in Garfield, New Jersey. The entire wedding party wore white for the lavish affair to symbolize new beginnings for the Jeans. "I think that as human beings, there will be mistakes," Jean told *Contact Music* about his past relationship missteps. "You grow from the mistakes."[68]

Clef and Cars

Wyclef Jean loves to spend his millions on cars. He owns nearly forty luxury vehicles that have been decked out in style. In addition to his Hummer with the built-in fish tank, Jean also owns a Pagani Zonda, a rare Italian sports car, and a McLaren F1, a racecar that can reach 231 mph (372kph). His collection also includes several motorcycles. One is custom decorated with silver spider-web rims and painted like Spiderman's costume.

In 2011, *Business Insider* named Jean's collection among the "Five Most Impressive Celebrity Car Collections." "Some people collect Picassos, I collect cars," he explains. "For me, the craftsmanship that goes into building vehicles like these is amazing. I love the artistry of it." He searches for specific rare cars and adds custom touches to all of his vehicles to reflect his personality.

Quoted in Frank Franklin II. "Wyclef Jean a Car Fanatic." *Chicago Tribune*. www.chicagotribune.com/sns-celebrity-jean-jpg,0,4336809.photo.

A Lavish Lifestyle

For Jean, advocating for the less fortunate in his songs did not mean he denied himself the spoils of his success. In addition to royalties on his own music, Jean was in high demand as a producer and that reflected in his paycheck. He produced not only R&B and hip-hop acts but also worked with singer Sinéad O'Connor and teamed up with Bono, front man for the best-selling rock band of all time, U2.

In 2005, Jean had a guest appearance on billionaire businessman Donald Trump's show *Celebrity Apprentice* and sees Trump as his investment mentor. Jean calls himself "The embodiment of the American dream"[69] because he grew up in the projects and is now worth $50 million. He sports diamond rings and often wears a diamond-studded lion's head around his neck. "It's the symbol of my spirituality,"[70] he says.

While Jean appreciates high fashion and flashy jewelry, his biggest indulgence is cars. He keeps his collection of nearly forty

Jean poses with one of his many luxury sports cars outside of his home in Saddle River, New Jersey, in 2005.

cars in a garage in Miami, including a Hummer with a built-in fish tank that Jean fills with sharks on special occasions. One of his favorite cars is a hot pink 1957 Cadillac Eldorado convertible with mink upholstery.

When not traveling in one of his custom-made cars, Jean has a private jet to whisk him to video shoots or concerts. He still lives in New Jersey but has moved to the leafy suburban town of Saddle River on a 2-acre estate (0.8ha) with a 6,500-square-foot house (604 sq. m) and a swimming pool. He also owns property in Miami Beach, Florida.

With a net worth of $50 million, Jean can afford indulgences like his car collection and beautiful homes, but he also wants to balance his extravagance with giving back to his community. While he has amassed this incredible wealth, he has never forgotten that he is "the Preacher's Son" and has an obligation to help those in need.

Chapter 5

Screaming for Haiti

Even as his wealth and fame grew, Wyclef Jean never lost his connection to his native country. In fact, he has never relinquished his Haitian citizenship to become a citizen of the United States. But Jean retains more than just a passport from his native land: He also feels a deep commitment to help his country escape poverty and environmental destruction. Since he was in the Fugees, Jean has been raising funds for and awareness of the situation in Haiti.

The Global Carnival

Jean began hosting benefit concerts to combat poverty in Haiti as early as 1997. Capitalizing on the success of *The Score*, Jean hosted a concert called "The Carnival" in Port-au-Prince meant to raise money for some twenty thousand Haitians who had been expelled from the Dominican Republic, where they had gone to work in the sugar industry. Unfortunately, a dispute arose after the concert and none of the money raised made its way to the refugees.

Undaunted, Jean decided to try again. The following year he moved The Carnival to Miami, Florida, a city with a sizeable Haitian immigrant population. He lined up more than a dozen acts, including the up-and-coming R&B group Destiny's Child, Beyoncé Knowles's original group. This time, the money went directly to his newly formed Wyclef Jean Foundation. The aim of the foundation was to provide musical instruments to Haitian children and sustain music education in public schools in America.

By 1999, Jean had expanded The Carnival's scope even further so that it also raised money to help refugees throughout the world. The 1999 concert, which featured names such as Bono and George Clinton, charged a thousand dollars per ticket to raise money to aid people affected by an ethnic conflict in Kosovo in the Balkans. Jean told Elena Oumano of *Billboard* that what he really wanted to do was create "a multibillion-dollar charity organization where we don't only focus on refugees in Haiti but globally, so I'm connected to everybody. . . . I'm crazy like that."[71]

Recognized for Giving Back

Another way Jean extended his philanthropy across the globe was to team up with NetAid, an organization that fights global poverty through partnerships between the United Nations and the private sector. In 1999, he collaborated with U2 front man Bono on a single called "New Day" that raised money for both NetAid and the Wyclef Jean Foundation. Jean and Bono performed the best-selling single live at the UN.

Because of his work raising money for various charitable causes, *Rolling Stone* awarded Jean a Do Something Award. In reflecting on

Bono and Jean perform at a concert to benefit NetAid in 1999. Their duet "New Day" raised money for both NetAid and Jean's own foundation.

the award, Jean remarked, "I don't want to be remembered as Mother Theresa or the Pope or anything, but I want to be remembered as someone who gave back to the kids."[72] Spurred by his desire to help children he started Clef's Kids, a (now-defunct) program that furnished talented music students with a new instrument, private lessons, and an opportunity to play with Jean at Carnegie Hall.

Some of the participants in Clef's Kids performed in that same January 2001 concert that Jean's father attended. In addition to being a personal milestone for Jean because it was the first time his father saw him perform, it was also an historic event for the venue. It was the first hip-hop festival held in the prestigious venue. Clef's Kids performed a number of songs, including one of Jean's favorites, "Lift Every Voice and Sing." The concert also featured Mary J. Blige, Destiny's Child, and Whitney Houston. Showing off his eclectic tastes, Jean also brought in a marching band and rearranged classical music to include hip-hop beats.

Clef in Cuffs

In 2002, Clef's activism was again on display when New York City mayor Michael Bloomberg proposed cutting the city's public school budget by an astonishing $356 million. At the same time, the teachers and the city were locked in a nineteen-month-long stalemate over a new contract. Celebrities, many of them products of New York City's public schools, protested the cuts and urged the city to negotiate a new contract with the teachers. The largest of such protests was organized by one of the founders of the hip-hop label Def Jam records, businessman Russell Simmons. Rap and R&B stars, including Jay-Z and Alicia Keyes, performed in front of a crowd of some twenty thousand, many of whom were students.

Jean was waiting to perform when he was surrounded by police and placed in handcuffs. Exactly what happened is not clear, but one eyewitness reported to the *New York Amsterdam News* that Jean was trying to get on stage, and the police thought he did not have a permit to perform. Jean lay face down on the sidewalk shouting, "I'm not leaving until I speak to the kids,"[73] according to a reporter from *Rolling Stone*.

Jean was only held for about three hours, but videos of the arrest sparked outrage and gave energy to a fledgling network of hip-hop activists. A week later, the teachers signed a new contract, but exactly how much influence the rappers had is up for debate. "I do not believe that Wyclef Jean really negotiated this contract," Mayor Bloomberg said, dismissing the effect of the video. But Randi Weingarten, president of the teacher's union, disagreed. "I believe [the rally] had an impact," she said. "It was a seminal event in New York City history."[74]

A Focus on Haiti

Even as Jean worked on behalf of New York City's public school students, he also continued to contribute to efforts to alleviate poverty in Haiti with concerts and fund-raisers. Wanting to focus more on his native country, in 2005 Jean created the Yéle Foundation, a nongovernmental organization, or NGO, originally meant to improve education for Haitian children. (NGOs are classified by the United Nations as organizations that are nonprofit and not part of the government of the country in which they operate.)

"Yéle is a word I created, a cry for freedom," Jean explained to Kathie Klarreich of *Time* magazine. The name sounds like the Haitian Creole word for "scream." He says the idea to create a foundation to help Haiti first came to him when he returned to Haiti with the Fugees in 1997. He remembers "smelling the air when I got off that plane, it felt like home."[75] His foundation began as the Yéle Center, an art school with a gymnasium, Internet café, and student exchange program. "When people are asking who is the next artist coming out, the next soccer player, or the next mathematician, I want them to be able to look at the Yéle Center,"[76] Jean told *Black Enterprise*.

Expanding to Meet Haiti's Needs

The foundation's activities quickly expanded to meet more of the needs of the residents of the poverty-stricken island. Created shortly after Tropical Storm Jeanne swept across Haiti in 2004, killing some three thousand people and destroying the homes and livelihoods of thousands more, Yéle mobilized food distribution

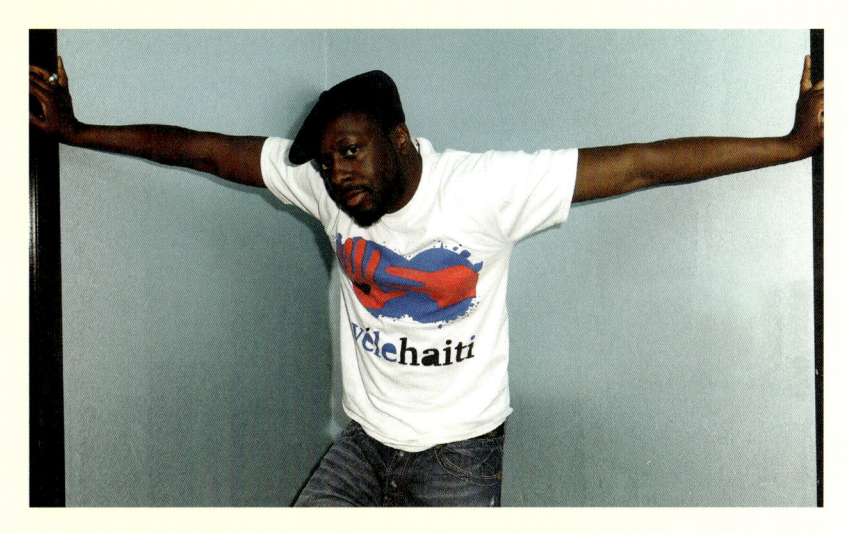

Jean wears a shirt promoting the Yéle Foundation, which he founded in 2005 to improve education for Haitian children.

and emergency relief as well as provided scholarships for students in the hardest-hit area. Jean said his foundation filled a void left by other organizations that did not understand what the country needed. "If something's not getting to the people, I go and get it to the people myself,"[77] Jean said in a special message recorded for YouTube, referring to his frustration with the lack of efficiency on the part of other NGOs.

The mission of the foundation expanded to include both emergency relief to communities dealing with natural disasters and developing long-term solutions to the country's most pressing problems: poverty, illiteracy, and lack of sustainable agriculture. In 2006, they started a program to employ individuals and provide them with vocational training, and in 2009 they began working to improve nutrition in Haiti's orphanages.

Big-Name Backers

As Yéle's work grew, they were able to tap into Jean's celebrity network for support. For example, in 2006 Angelina Jolie sold exclusive photos of herself pregnant to *People* magazine. She instructed

Jean is held up amid a crowd of people in Port-au-Prince while on a mission for his Yéle Foundation in 2006.

the magazine to send the nearly $1 million they paid her to Yéle. Other celebrity supporters include Eric Clapton and Matt Damon.

Yéle also teamed up with the Timberland clothing line to tackle one of Haiti's largest problems: deforestation. Beginning in the mid-1950s, logging companies cut down large swaths of Haiti's forest, while repeated hurricanes intensified tree loss. By 2005, only 2 percent of the nation's land was forested. Deforestation causes soil erosion, or soil loss, making farming more difficult. It also increases the frequency of devastating mudslides. Because of the erosion, it is difficult to farm in Haiti; the country imports 70 percent of its food—at enormous cost.

Jean and the Yéle Foundation decided to tackle this problem by working with farmers to increase their crop yields and incorporate better farming techniques into their enterprises. In addition, they started a campaign to reforest Haiti. In 2009, Jean signed a sponsorship agreement with the Timberland clothing company to help fund these endeavors. Timberland donated $2 from every pair of a special line of eco-friendly boots to the Yéle tree-planting program. In addition, they sold shirts designed by Haitian children and donated part of the proceeds to Yéle's school.

Yéle Takes Criticism

"The objective of Yéle Haiti is to restore pride and a reason to hope, and for the whole country to regain the deep spirit and strength that is part of our heritage,"[78] Jean explains in a statement about his foundation's lofty goals in regard to the Timberland deal. Yet to others, the objective of the Yéle Foundation seemed to be mainly about Jean's image. On his frequent visits to his native country, Jean was chauffeured in an SUV and accompanied by an entourage. Some NGO workers grumbled he looked more like a celebrity on his way to a club than a humanitarian.

For example, Maarten Boute, Belgian-born executive of Digicel Haiti, a Haitian cellphone company, expressed ambivalence about Jean's work to the *New York Times*. Boute, who has worked to change the Haitian economy with new technologies, praised some of Yéle's work. He was impressed with their emergency

Jean performs at a 2009 event celebrating his partnership with Timberland to fight deforestation in Haiti.

The Haitian Earthquake

Late in the afternoon on January 12, 2010, an earthquake occurred just 10 miles (15km) southwest of Port-au-Prince, Haiti. The earthquake registered a magnitude 7.0 and was one of the strongest the country had experienced in over two hundred years. Aftershocks continued to shake the capital for days after the initial quake.

People sit under a makeshift tent outside the damaged Presidential National Palace after an earthquake struck Haiti in January 2010.

According to the Red Cross, the earthquake affected at least 3 million people, or one-third of the population. The Haitian government estimated that some 316,000 people had died. Over a million people were left homeless, their poorly built neighborhoods reduced to rubble. National landmarks—the National Assembly, the Presidential National Palace, and the Port-au-Prince Cathedral—were severely damaged or completely destroyed.

With many of the country's hospitals and clinics partially or fully ruined, the injured struggled to find medical attention. Volunteers traveled to Haiti to help provide medical services, clear away debris, build transitional shelters and schools, and repair other buildings and churches. Volunteer police officers and military personnel tried to prevent looting and violence over food and other supplies but were not always successful. One boy working for Yéle Haiti was shot and killed in a carjacking. "It's something you just can't put into words," said Wyclef Jean as he reflected on the devastation of his homeland and Haitians' desperation to survive.

Quoted in Starpulse.com. "Wyclef Jean Volunteer Killed by Haitian Car-Jacker," January 31, 2010. www.starpulse.com/news/index.php/2010/01/31/wyclef_jean_volunteer_killed_by_haitian__1.

relief programs, particularly when they distributed rehydration kits during an outbreak of cholera, a disease that causes dehydration. But Boute added that Yéle does not try to "solve the problem at the roots." He also questioned Jean's reasons for his charity work, saying, "It's quite difficult . . . to really understand what are his real motivations."[79]

Yéle Under Fire

After an earthquake devastated Haiti in January 2010, Yéle went into high gear to provide relief. It—along with a number of other relief organizations—launched fund-raising campaigns in which people could donate through text messages. Tens of thousands of people texted, and the Yéle Foundation was expected to bring in more than $1 million per day. Within days of launching the campaign, however, the foundation faced accusations of cheating on its taxes and funneling money into its millionaire founder's pockets.

The Smoking Gun, a website that publishes leaked documents, obtained Yéle's tax returns and reported that the foundation had not filed tax documents until 2009, even though it had been in operation since 2005. In 2009, the organization filed back taxes for 2005, 2006, and 2007. Examinations of the documents raised questions. For example, the foundation paid Platinum Sound, Jean's recording studio, nearly $65,000 in rent over two years. In addition, they revealed that the organization paid Jean $100,000 for a benefit concert and wrote a $250,000 check to a Haitian television station owned by Jean's producing partner, Jerry Duplesis.

Jean Fires Back

At the time the allegations surfaced, Jean was in Haiti, providing earthquake assistance. In a recorded message distributed on YouTube, he defended his own work and the work of Yéle. "After digging kids up [from the rubble] and finding cemeteries to put them in, this is what I come back to: an attack on my integrity and my foundation," he said before adding that his commitment to his native land is "unprecedented."[80]

Screaming for Haiti

Haiti in His Own Words

Wyclef Jean saw many atrocities when he helped in Haiti after the 2010 earthquake. In an amateur video he shot of himself and his family helping survivors that was shown on *The Oprah Winfrey Show*, Jean described the following scene:

> Bone-chilling screams. It's the first sound my wife Claudette and I hear. . . . My entire hometown has become a morgue. . . . Everywhere we walked, bodies are abandoned in the streets. . . . We spent hours in the heat, piling up the dead. . . . The smell was overwhelming. . . . The local cemeteries are already overflowing so these survivors are digging shallow graves for the dead. Most of these people laid to rest here will never be identified. My team and I pulled this 14-year-old girl out of the rubble. She was trapped under part of her house. . . . There's so many dead bodies, every two corners you find at least 12 to 13 people. And then under the rubble . . . we don't even want to talk about it.

Quoted on Oprah.com. "Wyclef Jean's Tragic Trip Back to Haiti," January 20, 2010. www.oprah.com/oprahshow/Wyclef-Jeans-Tragic-Trip-Back-to-Haiti-Video.

Getting into greater specifics, he responded to the hundred-thousand-dollar price tag for the charity concert by saying, "You can't put a show together without a production. You need lights, you need a stage. . . . All of these things have to be accounted for."[81] He reminded viewers that he had contributed over $1 million of his own money to the organization and asked them to donate to the foundation so it could continue its relief work.

Despite his vigorous defense, criticism mounted as news organizations such as CNN and the *New York Times* covered the story. Charity Navigator, a watchdog group that rates nonprofits, refused to include Yéle in their listings because the foundation had not filed a sufficient number of tax documents. Ken Berger, chief executive of Charity Navigator, encouraged donors to "avoid this organization." He added, "What are the priorities of this organization? Is it really mission-driven, or is it more supporting the celebrity and financing him and his personal career?"[82]

Stepping Down

As the criticism grew, Jean recognized that the controversy was distracting from Yéle's work. After discussing his decision with Claudinette, Jean decided to step down from the organization and bring in a new accounting firm to look over the books. Jean announced his decision at a press conference in New York City, looking exhausted after spending three days in earthquake-ravaged Haiti. At one point, he addressed the cameras in Haitian Creole, tears streaming down his cheeks.

At the press conference, Jean admitted that the organization made mistakes but added, "Did I ever use any of Yéle's money for personal benefit, no. Yéle's books are open and transparent, and we have been [given] a clean bill of health by an external auditor every year since we started."[83] The organization made it through the scandal and managed to raise nearly $9 million to help fund their relief efforts in the aftermath of the earthquake. Jean himself remained dedicated to helping the island nation as well. "I am not stepping down in my commitment to Haiti,"[84] he clarified in a statement released a few months after the press conference.

Remaking a Classic

Jean showed his commitment to Haiti by helping to organize an enormous gathering of superstar recording artists to record a version of the 1985 hit "We Are the World" to raise money for relief work. The song was originally written by R&B singer-songwriter Lionel Richie and pop star Michael Jackson as a charity single for African famine relief. Jackson and Richie's version was one of the fewer than thirty singles in the history of pop to sell over 10 million copies.

Jean hoped to replicate the success of the original on its twenty-fifth anniversary but also provide it with a fresh sound. Working with Richie, producer Quincy Jones, and a crew of

Singers including, from left, Gladys Knight, Celine Dion, Justin Bieber, Tony Braxton, and Usher joined Jean in 2010 to record an updated version of "We Are the World."

younger producers, Jean kept the structure of the original but added rap verses and incorporated some of Jackson's parts from the 1985 recording. (Jackson had died a few months prior.) Eighty-five singers and rappers contributed their talents, including eighty-three-year-old crooner Tony Bennett and teenage pop sensation Justin Bieber. Jean sings part of a chorus in Creole. The song premiered during the opening ceremony for the 2010 Winter Olympics, and the money it raised created a new charity organization: The We Are the World Foundation.

With his native country buried under the rubble and his foundation's survival dependent on him distancing himself from it, Jean needed to find another way to make a real difference in Haiti. After stepping down from Yéle, he had vowed "regardless of what path I take next, one thing is certain: My focus on helping Haiti turn a new corner will only grow stronger."[85] Jean wanted to do more than record charity singles and considered how he could best help his country grow.

Chapter 6

Clef for President

In the year following the earthquake, Wyclef Jean continued to return to Haiti to volunteer and coordinate relief efforts. There he saw a country with no clear plan to tackle the problem of tens of thousands of people living in refugee camps and tent cities. He knew the nation needed more than emergency aid; it needed systemic reforms to lift it from decades of poverty and political corruption. Jean believed he could implement those reforms as the nation's president.

Goodwill Ambassador

To many, a hip-hop star running for president raised eyebrows: They questioned whether a celebrity had the kind of experience that running a country requires. But Jean had been involved in Haitian politics for about five years. For example, in 2005, the United States government limited the amount of clothing Haiti could export to America and more than eighty thousand Haitians working in the garment industry lost their jobs. Jean joined his uncle Raymond Joseph, who served as the Haitian ambassador, and a delegation of Haitian government and industry leaders to lobby Congress to lift the regulations.

Impressed by Jean's success in Washington, Haitian president René Préval named Jean a roving ambassador for Haiti. As an ambassador, Jean was tasked with traveling internationally to promote the country's image. "We have so much to recover from with our bad reputation," Foreign Affairs Minister Rénald Clérismé told *USA Today*. "With Wyclef, we can gain a lot."[86] A year later,

Political Corruption in Haiti

When Jean entered the presidential election, he waded into the political process of a country marked by corruption since the moment of its independence. In 1804, Haiti declared itself a democracy but has since been ruled by a number of dictators. Throughout the latter half of the twentieth century, the Duvaliers controlled the country with an iron fist. In 1957 François "Papa Doc" Duvalier won a rigged election and in 1964 declared himself president for life. His son, Jean-Claude "Baby Doc" Duvalier, inherited the presidency in 1971.

A man destroys a photo of Haitian president Jean-Claude Duvalier during a riot in 1985.

In February 1986, a coup forced the younger Duvalier out of the country, and a new constitution was instated by popular vote in 1987. Jean-Bertrand Aristide won the 1990 election and chose René Préval as his prime minister. This new regime did not last long before a violent coup led by General Raoul Cedras chased Aristide from Haiti; it was not until 1994 that the UN Security Council acted on Aristide's behalf and forced Cedras out.

Despite Aristide's initial popularity, his government was criticized for inefficacy and rigged elections. A 2004 coup removed him from office, and Préval was elected in 2006. Several presidencies have followed over the years, each one marred by either crime or ineptitude. This legacy of corruption and ineffectiveness is part of what motivated Jean to run for president in 2010.

Jean became a goodwill ambassador, a position that also involved promoting Haitian business and culture.

At the time of the January 2010 earthquake, Jean was still an ambassador. The day after the quake, Jean flew to Haiti and met with President Préval to survey the devastation. "I looked into Préval's eyes, which were anguished. And he said, '. . . It's the apocalypse,'" Jean told Douglas Brinkley of *Rolling Stone*. "Everything was so bad. Everything was broken. It was a body blow hard to put into words."[87]

Jean immediately threw himself into relief efforts, searching the rubble for the dead and trying to find cemeteries for the mounting number of casualties. "He was one of the first people on the ground," his brother Samuel says. "He said, 'I couldn't sleep with myself if I just walked away from this. . . . You can raise money, you can raise awareness, but there comes a point where you've pushed that as far as it can go.'"[88] As Jean worked in the rubble, he began to think he could do more for his country than use his celebrity to get people to write checks. He had ideas about systemic reforms and national programs.

Presidential Announcement

The Haitian presidential election had been postponed due to the quake, and in the summer of 2010 candidates began campaigning for the country's highest office. With his schedule cleared after stepping down from the Yéle Foundation, Jean considered joining the crowded field of some thirty candidates, including the current president, Préval, and his own uncle, Raymond Joseph. It would mean running against a family member and a long-time supporter—after all it was Préval who named Jean ambassador.

Ultimately, Jean decided it was worth potential bruised feelings. On August 5, 2010, he formally announced he was running for president of Haiti for the Viv Ansamm ("Live Together") Party. He outlined his platform, which included improving education, combating unemployment, and promoting Haitian agriculture. "I am running for president because this little nation with big problems and even bigger heart can no longer wait to turn a corner,"[89] he

Jean speaks to reporters in Port-au-Prince after submitting paperwork to run for president in Haiti in August 2010.

declared. Recognizing his lack of experience, Jean gathered a team of knowledgeable advisers, including Kerry Kennedy, the daughter of Robert Kennedy, the former New York senator who was assassinated during a bid for the U.S. presidency in 1968.

Jean appointed his brother Samuel as his campaign spokesman, a position that required him to put a positive spin on Jean running against his uncle. "We have a lot of respect for Uncle Ray," the younger Jean told Stephen Kurczy of the *Christian Science Monitor*. "I don't think they perceive it as running against each other. . . . The Haitian people, the more choices they have, the better chance they have of making a good selection."[90]

A Youth Campaign

Unsurprisingly, Jean enjoyed massive support from the population, who already saw him as a symbol of national pride. He was especially beloved by young people. Jean was unafraid to travel into slums controlled by violent gangs and talk directly to young people about their lives. He spoke about how their choices can affect the country and encouraged them to set aside gang wars to work together to improve conditions in the slum. His campaign slogan, "jen kore jen," roughly translates as "youth strengthen youth."[91]

While he waded into the slums to campaign, he set up offices in the opulent National Palace in Port-au-Prince, an act criticized as arrogant. Journalist Douglas Brinkley describes Jean as "deeply learned in Haitian history, and imbued with an almost surreal self-confidence."[92] The hip-hop star drew from the Bible to frame his campaign. He likened himself to Moses, the biblical prophet who returned from exile to liberate his people from their bondage to the Egyptians. As a baby, Moses was placed in a basket and hidden in the bulrushes of the Nile River by his mother to avoid being killed by the Egyptians. Later, God spoke to him in the form of a burning bush. Jean described his journey to presidential bid as going "from my basket in the bulrushes to standing in front of the burning bush. I knew I'd have to take the next step."[93]

"Flaky Performance Art"

While Jean saw himself as akin to a biblical figure, others were not as impressed. Tim Padgett remarked in *Time*, "It's tempting to dismiss [Jean's campaign] as flaky performance art, a publicity stunt from the same guy who just a few years ago recorded a number called 'If I Was President.'"[94] Many asked what a musician could contribute to politics. "If I can't take five years out to serve my country as president," Jean fired back, "then everything I've been singing about, like equal rights, doesn't mean anything."[95]

He also suffered personal attacks from friends. His former bandmate Pras Michel publically declared he would never vote for Jean. He said Jean lacked experience and compared him with Sarah Palin, the inexperienced 2008 Republican vice presidential candidate who had become the butt of jokes on late-night comedy.

Actor Sean Penn, who was intimately involved in Haitian relief efforts, publically questioned Jean's motives and his ties to American corporations that exploited Haiti for cheap labor. Penn was disturbed by Jean's flashy appearances. He told CNN, "I want to see someone who's really, really willing to sacrifice for their country, and not just someone who I personally saw with a vulgar entourage of vehicles that demonstrated a wealth in Haiti that, in context, I felt was a very obscene demonstration."[96]

Knocked Out of the Race

Meanwhile, it was revealed that Jean owed more than $5 million in back taxes to the United States government. Others lambasted Jean for being a poor role model because he had produced songs about taking drugs and was a former petty criminal and a notorious partier. "He's always been honest about what he has done, the culture and lifestyle he has," Sam Jean said in defense of his brother. "He's never promoted for people to do the things he's done that he's not proud of."[97]

While Jean could combat criticism that he lacked experience by pointing to his team of advisers, there was nothing he could do in the face of allegations that he was unqualified to run because he did not meet residency requirements. The truth was, Jean did not

Jean awaits word on his eligibility to run for president of Haiti. Election officials determined that Jean could not run because he was not a resident of Haiti.

live in Haiti. Despite his citizenship and Haitian passport, Jean was a full-time resident of the United States. Less than a month after he announced his candidacy, election officials barred him from running. Jean's legal team disputed their decision, but to no avail.

Jean was disappointed at the ruling but refused to walk away from his native country. He appealed the ruling, stating, "It's not about my candidacy—this appeal was meant to address the shortcomings of the process for every Haitian," adding, "Though my run for the presidency was cut short, in this way, I feel it was not in vain; it's something we can use to improve conditions for my Haitian brothers and sisters."[98]

He decided to use his celebrity to back a candidate who shared his vision. He therefore endorsed Michel Martelly, another musician in the race. Jean spent a lot of time in Haiti campaigning for Martelly. While the candidate would open events with one of his own songs and a speech, the crowd was always there more to see Jean and erupted into cheers and applause when he appeared onstage. Jean vowed to stay involved in Haitian politics as an ambassador or adviser to the president.

The Dangers of the Campaign Trail

As he campaigned for Martelly and continued his fund-raising efforts, Jean felt guilty about not being home with his family. He missed his daughter's sixth birthday, managing only to reach her by phone to sing "Happy Birthday" in the car between campaign events. But there were other dangers as well. Haiti was in chaos and crime was rampant, especially in the slums where Jean campaigned. When Jean organized a campaign rally for Martelly that included an appearance by American rapper Busta Rhymes, Rhymes was robbed at the concert.

In March, Jean was nearly shot while standing near his car. He told reporter Anand Giridharadas that his entourage had stopped because someone needed to use the bathroom. While waiting, he heard gunshots and a bullet grazed his hand. Later, however, even this claim came under attack when Giridharadas obtained a medical report that seemed to suggest that Jean's hand was merely cut on broken glass.

Jean uses an injured hand to cast a ballot in Haiti's presidential election in March 2011.

Although details of the shooting were murky, to Jean, the actual facts of the story were less important than its effect. He told *People* magazine that the incident brought attention to the election going on in Haiti—something most of the world would not otherwise be aware of. "The story is about the fact that we had an election and our party is in the lead," he said. "It's a young party, trying to take over the country,"[99] he added, turning the incident into a story about how those in power wanted to keep fresh blood out of politics. In the following weeks, he performed with his injured hand wrapped in a Haitian flag.

Though he emerged from the incident safely, there was no doubt that Jean was putting himself in danger by traveling in a chaotic country plagued by violence. However, he refused to slow down or stop his work there. "You have two choices—either sit back thinking of the danger or do something to move your country forward,"[100] he told Martin Fletcher of the London *Times*. Jean chose the second option and continued campaigning for Martelly, who won the election and was sworn in as president on May 14, 2011.

Did Wyclef Predict His Assassination Attempt?

On July 15, 2008, Jean released a single called "If I Was President," which he performed live on the popular comedy show *The Chappelle Show*. The song was written during the presidential contest between Barack Obama and John McCain. On the track, Jean sings that if he were elected president, he would trade military funding for antipoverty efforts and create unity among religious groups. He also sang that he would have to watch for snipers because he would be killed on his first day in office. In 2010, when reports surfaced that Jean had survived an "assassination attempt" during the campaign for the Haitian presidency, reporters cited his 2008 single as an eerie prediction of the violence he had experienced.

Stretched Too Thin

With all his work campaigning, Jean had less time for his music. In September 2009, he announced that he had started work on his eighth album, called *If I Was President*, but progress on the record slowed as Jean kept returning to Haiti. After failing to make it onto the ballot for the presidential election, Jean wrote on his blog that he would return to the studio to finish the album.

In September 2010, however, all work came to a halt when Jean was hospitalized for exhaustion. "Wyclef Jean has had an extremely grueling three months," his publicist, Marian Salzman, told the press. "Truly an exhausting eight months, since the earthquake when he recommitted himself to our homeland and his passion for our people."[101] After being released from the hospital, Jean returned home to rest.

Feeling exhausted from his near-constant travel, Jean decided not to finish a full album. Instead he digitally released a six-song extended play recording, or EP. The EP focused on Jean's travel to and work in Haiti. It included songs like "Earthquake," that featured Jean singing over acoustic instruments about the evils of environmental destruction, income inequality, and war. He also sings about how Haiti needs jobs, agriculture, business, and—of course—music. The videos that accompanied the EP showed Jean strumming a guitar in the streets of Haiti, and young Haitians dancing and singing together. The EP exuded a surprising optimism about the country given all that Jean has seen and experienced there.

Do Not Forget Haiti

Jean began 2011 completely recovered from his grueling campaign and ready to re-commit both to Haiti and to his music. Shortly after his election, President Martelly reappointed Jean as a goodwill ambassador, and Jean resumed his work promoting Haiti abroad. In July, Martelly further honored Jean by naming him Grand Officer of the National Order of Honor and Merit. It is the highest possible honor a person can receive from the Haitian government. "I have great joy in solemnly honoring a son of this earth who has assumed with force, conviction and humanity, his Haitian quality," Martelly said at the ceremony before adding: "You are one of the Haitians who make us proud."[102]

On the two-year anniversary of the earthquake, Jean returned to Haiti to mark the occasion. He filmed a special report on the country for *106 and Park*, a popular show on Black Entertainment Television (BET). In the special, he urged viewers not to forget the devastation that the country had experienced and reminded them that the island was still in great need of assistance. He spent the day of the anniversary meeting with reporters, volunteering, and talking with citizens.

Moving Forward, Feeling Good

As of 2012, Jean was working on his ninth studio album called *Feel Good Music*. On this album, listeners can expect more eclectic music and collaborations with artists from many genres. "It's just

Haitian president Michel Martelly presents Jean as a Grand Officer of the National Order of Honor and Merit at a ceremony in July 2011.

[that] you could never define me or put me in a box," Jean told MTV when announcing the album. He has been working on it since summer 2011, but says an album of this kind cannot be rushed. "My albums, you have to listen to them from beginning to end. It's going to be like a stage play, but it's definitely going to feel good,"[103] he said.

The musician did not wait for the album to come out to resume touring, and in 2012 played at a number of high profile venues. He kicked off the year with a show at the famous Bellagio hotel and casino in Las Vegas and performed the half-time show at an NBA game between the Detroit Pistons and Sacramento Kings in February.

Jean has come a long way from a barefoot boy watching mermaids off the coast of Haiti. He is partially responsible for the history-making album *The Score* and is a multiplatinum

Clef for President **83**

Jean performs an outdoor concert in New York City in 2012, one of several live gigs he played that year while working on his ninth studio album.

recording artist in his own right. He has become a symbol of Haitian national pride and a generous philanthropist, but—as he made clear when talking about his new album—his music is still rooted in the rhythms of his native island.

Notes

Introduction: Who Is Wyclef Jean?

1. Alec Foege. "Fugees: Leaders of the New Cool." *Rolling Stone*, September 5, 1996, p. 42.
2. Quoted in Pete Lewis. "Wyclef Jean: Perfect Gentleman." *Blues and Soul*, Winter 2012 www.bluesandsoul.com/feature/360/wyclef_jean_perfect_gentleman.
3. Quoted in Kathie Klarreich. "Q&A: Wycelf Jean." *Time*, November 26, 2006. www.time.com/time/magazine/article/0,9171,1562954,00.html.
4. Tim Padgett. "Wyclef Jean to Run for President of Haiti." *Time*, August 4, 2010. www.time.com/time/magazine/article/0,9171,2008893,00.html.
5. Quoted in Big Think. "Big Think Interview with Wyclef Jean," July 24, 2009. www.bigthink.com/ideas/15601.

Chapter 1: A City of Diamonds, a City of Beats

6. Quoted in Gavin Edwards. "Rapper, Hipster, Huckster, Preacherman, Lover Boy, Thug Angel, Country Aficionado, Wresting Fan, Global Visionary . . . Wyclef Is All These Things and More." *Rolling Stone*, October 12, 2000, p. 48.
7. Quoted in Edwards, "Rapper, Hipster, Huckster, . . . ," p. 48.
8. Quoted in Edwards, "Rapper, Hipster, Huckster, . . . ," p. 48.
9. Quoted in Big Think. "Big Think Interview with Wyclef Jean."
10. Quoted in Melissa Ewey. "Wyclef's World." *Ebony*, May 1998, p. 120.
11. Quoted in Steven Baker and Julia Hoppock. "*Nightline* Playlist: Wyclef Jean." ABC News, December 8, 2007. www.abcnews.go.com/Nightline/story?id=3969239.

12. Quoted in Ewey. "Wyclef's World," p. 120.
13. Quoted in Edwards. "Rapper, Hipster, Huckster, . . . ," p. 48.
14. Quoted in Louise Gannon. "Wyclef Jean: He's Gone from Robbing a Store at Gunpoint, to Global Superstar." *Mail Online*, November 10, 2007. www.dailymail.co.uk/home/moslive/article-491341/Wyclef-Jean-Hes-gone-robbing-store-gunpoint-global-superstar.html.
15. Quoted in Gannon. "Wyclef Jean."
16. Quoted in Gannon. "Wyclef Jean."
17. The Boombox. "Interview with Wyclef Jean by Citizens School Students," December 16, 2010. www.theboombox.com/2010/12/16/citizen-schools-students-interview-wyclef-jean.
18. Quoted in CBS News. "Wyclef Jean's Hopes for Haiti," August 2, 2009. www.cbsnews.com/2100-18560_162-4707723.html.
19. Quoted in Baker and Hoppock. "*Nightline* Playlist."
20. Quoted in Big Think. "Big Think Interview with Wyclef Jean."

Chapter 2: Straight from the Booga Basement

21. Quoted in Foege, "Fugees," pg. 40.
22. Quoted in Edwards, "Rapper, Hipster, Huckster, . . .," p. 48.
23. Quoted in Foege, "Fugees," p. 40.
24. Jason Birchmeier. "Review of *Blunted on Reality*." AllMusic. www.allmusic.com/album/blunted-on-reality-r203134/review.
25. Quoted in Foege. "Fugees," p. 40.
26. Quoted in Muriel L. Whetstone. "The Fugees: Erasing Cultural Barriers." *Ebony*, November 1996, p. 72.
27. Foege. "Fugees," p. 40.
28. Whetstone. "The Fugees," p. 72.
29. Quoted in Christopher John Farley. "Not Your Father's Hip-Hop." *Time*, February 12, 1996, p. 79.

30. Quoted in Foege. "Fugees," p. 40.
31. Quoted in Amy Linden. "With a Little Help from Roberta Flack, the Fugees Are Redefining Rap." *New York Times*, May 26, 1996, p. 24.
32. Quoted in Linden. "With a Little Help from Roberta Flack, the Fugees are Redefining Rap," p. 24.
33. Whetstone. "The Fugees," p. 74.

Chapter 3: Flying Solo

34. Quoted in Steve Dougherty. "A Different Beat." *People*, December 8, 2003. www.people.com/people/archive/article/0,,20148883,00.html.
35. Quoted in Neil Strauss. "Return of a Haitian Prodigal: For a Rap Leader, a Concert Grows into a State Visit." *New York Times*, April 15, 1997, p. 11.
36. Quoted in Garry Pierre-Pierre. "Hip-Hop Idol Is the Pride of a People; Young Haitian-Americans Get Help Against Stigma." *New York Times*, March 28, 1998, p. B6.
37. Quoted in Pierre-Pierre. "Hip-Hop Idol Is the Pride of a People," p. B6.
38. Quoted in Dougherty. "A Different Beat."
39. Quoted in Havelock Nelson. "Columbia Plans Global Blitz for New Solo Set from Fugees' Wyclef," *Billboard*, June 14, 1997, p. 1.
40. James Rotondi. "Wyclef Jean: Hip Hop's First Guitar Hero." *Guitar Player*, January 1998, p. 35.
41. Quoted in DimeWars. "Interview with Wyclef Jean" (video). www.dimewars.com/Video/Wyclef-Jean-Explains-His-Side-Of-The-Fugees-Break-Up-Story.aspx?bcmediaid=561b7885-2144-4746-9201-6cb12d2d5f34&activetab=1.
42. Quoted in Rashaun Hall. "Wyclef Jean Goes 'Ecleftic' on Columbia." *Billboard*, July 8, 2000, p. 1.
43. Quoted in Farley. "Wyclef's World," p. 72.
44. Quoted in Farley. "Wyclef's World," p. 72.
45. Quoted in Farley. "Wyclef's World," p. 72.

46. Nathan Rabin. "Wyclef Jean: *Masquerade*." *A.V. Club*, July 22, 2002. www.avclub.com/articles/wyclef-jean-masquerade,17263.
47. Sal Cinquemani. "Wyclef Jean: *Masquerade*." *Slant Magazine*, June 17, 2002. www.slantmagazine.com/music/review/wyclef-jean-masquerade/99.
48. Quoted in Dougherty. "A Different Beat."
49. Quoted in DimeWars. "Interview with Wyclef Jean."
50. Quoted in DimeWars. "Interview with Wyclef Jean."
51. Quoted in Farley. "Wyclef's World," p. 72.
52. Quoted in Dougherty. "A Different Beat."
53. Quoted in Edwards. "Rapper, Hipster, Huckster, . . . , " p. 48.

Chapter 4: Clef, the Songwriter

54. Stephen Kurczy. "Wyclef Jean: Preacher's Son to Rap Star to Presidential Contender." *Christian Science Monitor*, August 6, 2010. www.csmonitor.com/World/Americas/2010/0806/Wyclef-Jean-Preacher-s-son-to-rap-star-to-presidential-contender.
55. Julia Llewellyn Smith. "Mr. High and Mighty." *Daily Telegraph* (London), November 14, 2003. www.telegraph.co.uk/culture/music/3606771/Mr-High-and-Mighty.html.
56. Quoted in Dougherty. "A Different Beat."
57. Quoted in Hall. "New Label Fits Jean Fine." *Billboard*, November 8, 2003, p. 16.
58. Rob Theakston. "Review: *The Preacher's Son*." AllMusic. www.allmusic.com/album/the-preachers-son-r659576/review.
59. Michael Paoletta. "*The Preacher's Son* (Music)." *Billboard*, November 15, 2003, p. 22.
60. Quoted in Hall. "New Label Fits Jean Fine," p. 16.
61. Quoted in Ernie Rideout, "In the 'Clef Zone'—for Wyclef Jean, Hip-Hop Citizen of the World, This Is Just the Beginning, " *Keyboard,* August 1, 2003, p. 26.
62. Quoted in Dougherty. "A Different Beat."

63. Wyclef Jean. "Message of Hope Arises from the Rwandan Devastation: Making a Difference." *Billboard*, February 19, 2005, p. 10.
64. Quoted in Lewis. "Wyclef Jean: Perfect Gentleman."
65. Quoted in Lewis. "Wyclef Jean: Perfect Gentleman."
66. Steve Juon. "Wyclef Jean: *Carnival Vol. II: Memoirs of an Immigrant*." Rap Reviews.com, December 4, 2007. www.rapreviews.com/archive/2007_12_carnival2.html.
67. Kelefa Sanneh. "Critics Choice: New CDs: Wyclef Jean 'Carnival II: Memoirs of an Immigrant.'" *New York Times*, December 3, 2007, p. E3.
68. Contactmusic.com. "Wyclef and Wife Renew Vows," August 31, 2009. www.contactmusic.com/news/wyclef-and-wife-renew-vows_1114517.
69. Quoted in Smith. "Mr. High and Mighty."
70. Quoted in Smith. "Mr. High and Mighty."

Chapter 5: Screaming for Haiti

71. Quoted in Elena Oumano. "Wyclef Jean Foundation Plans Fundraiser." *Billboard*, March 21, 1998, p. 35.
72. Quoted in John Gill. "Wyclef to Be Honored for Charitable Efforts," MTV.com, October 28, 1999. www.mtv.com/news/articles/1429168/wyclef-be-honored-charitable-efforts.jhtml.
73. Quoted in Warren Cohen. "Wyclef Arrested." *Rolling Stone*, July 25, 2002, p. 22.
74. Quoted in Cohen. "Wyclef Arrested," p. 22.
75. Quoted in Klarreich. "Q & A: Wyclef Jean," p. 129.
76. Quoted in LaToya M. Smith. "Backtalk with Wyclef Jean." *Black Enterprise*, January 2010, p. 104.
77. Wyclef Jean, "Wyclef's Personal Statement on the Accusations Against Yéle Haiti" (video). *VLADTV*, January 16, 2010. www.vladtv.com/video/15591/wyclefs-personal-statement-on-the-accusations-against-yele-haiti.
78. Quoted in David DeFranza. "Help Wyclef Jean and Timberland Reforest Haiti." *Planet Green*, October 2, 2009.

www.planetgreen.discovery.com/fashion-beauty/wyclef-jean-timberland-haiti.html.
79. Quoted in Anand Giridharadas. "The Would-Be Prince of Port-au-Prince." *New York Times*, July 15, 2011. www.nytimes.com/2011/07/17/magazine/what-is-wyclef-jean-trying-to-save-in-haiti.html.
80. Wyclef Jean. "Wyclef's Personal Statement on the Accusations Against Yele Haiti."
81. Quoted in Karen Pantelides. "Wyclef Jean Defends Yele Haiti." CNN Money, January 17, 2010. www.money.cnn.com/2010/01/17/news/international/Yele_Haiti/index.htm.
82. Quoted in Giridharadas. "The Would-Be Prince of Port-au-Prince."
83. Quoted in Jayson Rodriguez. "Wyclef Jean Defends Yele Haiti at Emotional NYC Press Conference." *Rolling Stone*, January 18, 2010. www.rollingstone.com/music/news/wyclef-jean-defends-yele-haiti-at-emotional-nyc-press-conference-20100118.
84. Quoted in Associated Press. "Wyclef Jean Resigns from Yele Before Presidential Run," *News One*, August 5, 2010. www.newsone.com/world/associated-press/wyclef-jean-resigns-from-yele-before-presidential-run.
85. Quoted in Associated Press. "Wyclef Jean Resigns from Yele Before Presidential Run."

Chapter 6: Clef for President

86. Quoted in Associated Press. "Wyclef Jean Is Named Haiti 'Ambassador.'" *USA Today*, January 4, 2007. www.usatoday.com/life/people/2007-01-04-wyclef-haiti_x.htm.
87. Quoted in Dougas Brinkley. "Wyclef's Mission." *Rolling Stone*, September 2, 2010, p. 50.
88. Quoted in Kurczy. "Wyclef Jean."
89. Wyclef Jean. "My Vision for Haiti." *Wall Street Journal*, August 7, 2010, p. A13.
90. Quoted in Kurczy. "Wyclef Jean."

91. Allyn Gaestel. "Who Will Be Haiti's Next President?" *Boston Haitian Reporter*, November 10, 2010. www.bostonhaitian.com/2010/who-will-be-haiti's-next-president.
92. Brinkley. "Wyclef's Mission," p. 50.
93. Quoted in Padgett. "Wyclef Jean to Run for President of Haiti."
94. Padgett. "Wyclef Jean to Run for President of Haiti."
95. Quoted in Padgett. "Wyclef Jean to Run for President of Haiti."
96. Quoted in *Larry King Live*. "Sean Penn Skeptical of Wyclef Jean." Video. CNN, August 5, 2010. www.cnn.com/video/?/video/bestoftv/2010/08/05/lkl.sean.penn.cnn.
97. Quoted in Kurczy. "Wyclef Jean."
98. Wyclef Jean. "Statement from Wyclef Jean," September 22, 2010. www.wyclefjean.wordpress.com/2010/09/22/statement-from-wyclef-jean.
99. Quoted in Mark Grey. "Wyclef Jean: I Felt 'Shock and Awe' when I was shot." *People*, March 28, 2011. www.people.com/people/article/0,,20476874,00.html.
100. Quoted in Martin Fletcher. "Wyclef Jean: I Could Be Killed Standing for Haiti Presidency." *Times* (London), August 7, 2010, p. 38.
101. Quoted in Andrew Kerr. "Wyclef Jean Treated for Exhaustion in Hospital." *Spinner*, September 28, 2010. www.spinner.com/2010/09/28/wyclef-jean-exhaustion-hospital.
102. Quoted in Tim Saunders. "Wyclef Jean Honored for Charity Work in Haiti." Look to the Stars, July 22, 2011. www.looktothestars.org/news/6658-wyclef-jean-honored-for-charity-work-in-haiti.
103. Quoted in Rob Markman. "Wyclef to Make *Feel Good Music* on Next Album," MTV.com, July 12, 2011. www.mtv.com/news/articles/1667169/wyclef-feel-good-music-album.jhtml.

Important Dates

1969

Nelust Wyclef Jean is born on October 17 in Croix-des-Bouquets, Haiti.

1979

Jean immigrates to the United States and joins parents in Brooklyn, New York.

1982

Jean moves with family to Newark, New Jersey, where his father, the Reverend Gesner Jean, serves as the pastor of Good Shepherd Church of the Nazarene.

1987

While studying jazz at Valisburg High School, Jean joins hip-hop experimental group known as Tranzlator Crew started by his friend Prakazrel "Pras" Michel and Lauryn Hill.

1993

Tranzlator Crew is signed to Ruffhouse/Columbia Records as the Fugees.

1994

The Fugees release debut album, *Blunted on Reality* (Ruffhouse/Columbia Records), on February 1. Jean marries fashion designer Marie Claudinette on August 9.

1996

The Fugees release second album, *The Score* (Ruffhouse/Columbia Records), on February 13; Refugee Camp Youth Project is founded.

1997

The Fugees win two Grammy Awards for Best Rap Album (*The Score*) and Best R&B Vocal Performance by a Duo or Group ("Killing Me Softly"). Wyclef releases first solo project, *Wyclef Jean Presents the Carnival Featuring the Refugee All-Stars* (Ruffhouse/Columbia Records), on June 24. *The Score* is certified six times platinum by the RIAA on October 3.

1998

Jean is nominated for a Grammy for Best Rap Album for *The Carnival*. Starts Wyclef Jean Foundation.

2000

Jean releases *The Ecleftic: 2 Sides II a Book* (Columbia Records) on July 25; nominated for MTV Europe Music Award for Best Hip-Hop Act. Produces "Maria Maria" by Santana, which hits number one on U.S. *Billboard* Hot 100 and Hot R&B/Hip-Hop Songs.

2001

Gesner Jean dies in an accident in September.

2002

Jean is arrested at a June rally against budget cuts to the New York Public School system. Releases *Masquerade* (Columbia Records) on July 18.

2003

Jean releases *The Preacher's Son* (J-Records) on November 4, in memory of his father.

2004

Jean's song "Million Voices" is released on the film soundtrack for *Hotel Rwanda*. The Fugees briefly reunite in September to perform in Dave Chappelle's Block Party concert in Brooklyn. Jean releases *Welcome to Haiti: Creole 101* (Koch Records) on October 5.

2005

Jean and Claudinette adopt daughter, Angelina Claudinette Jean. Starts Yéle Haiti Foundation, while his uncle, Raymond Alcide Joseph, becomes Haitian ambassador to the United States. Acts in NBC's *Third Watch*. Wins Golden Satellite Award for Best Original Song for "Million Voices" and is nominated for a Golden Globe Award for Best Original Song for a Motion Picture. Performs with the Fugees at BET's 2005 Music Awards in June and goes on tour in Europe with the group from November 30 to December 20.

2006

Jean contributes to Shakira's recording of "Hips Don't Lie," which becomes an international number one hit and the most-played pop song over a single week (ending June 2) according to Nielsen Broadcast Data Systems; "Million Voices" is nominated for Grammy Award for Best Song Written for a Motion Picture, Television, or Other Visual Media.

2007

Jean named roving ambassador to Haiti by Haitian president René Préval. Releases *Carnival Vol. II: Memoirs of an Immigrant* (Sony) on December 4.

2009

Jean enrolls at Berklee College of Music. Hosts and performs at the MTV Africa Music Awards in Nairobi, Kenya, in October. Releases *Toussaint St. Jean: From the Hut, to the Projects, to the Mansion* (Columbia Records) on November 10.

2010

Jean produces "We Are the World 25 for Haiti" with Quincy Jones and Lionel Richie in an effort to raise awareness of Haiti's devastation after a massive earthquake in January. Awarded honorary doctorate from Western Connecticut State University. Resigns as board member and chairman of Yéle Haiti and on August 5 announces bid for candidacy in the 2010 Haitian presidential election, but is found ineligible according to rules of residency; candidacy is rejected on August 20. Releases online EP, *If I Were President: My Haitian Experience* (Columbia Records), on December 3.

2011

Rumors surface in March of an alleged shooting of Jean in Haiti, but according to medical reports he is only wounded in the hand by glass. Announces plans for his next album, *Feel Good Music*.

2012

Jean returns to Haiti for a day of volunteer work to mark the anniversary of the earthquake.

For More Information

Books

Chad Bonham. "The Preacher's Son." In *Spiritual Journeys: How Faith Has Influenced Twelve Music Icons*. Lake Mary, FL: Relevant Books, 2003. A collection of essays on twelve musicians' spiritual influences, including a chapter on Wyclef Jean, Lauryn Hill, and some of Jean's musical role models.

Jana Evans Braziel. *Artists, Performers, and Black Masculinity in the Haitian Diaspora*. Bloomington: Indiana University Press, 2008. A book about male artists from Haiti in America, explored through the Haitian Creole concept of gwo nègs, or "big men." Features a chapter on Wyclef Jean.

Jacques Guillaume and Jean Jocelyn. *Haiti, Wyclef Jean & The Scavengers*. Bloomington, IN: iUniverse, 2011. Examines Haiti's controversial political structure, the disenfranchisement of voters, and Wyclef Jean's presidential campaign up to his post-disqualification endorsement of Michel Martelly for president.

Chris Roberts. *Fugees*. London: Virgin, 1998. Follows the Fugees' rise to fame, from their signing to Sony Records to their success after *The Score*; the book also provides profiles on the band's members and examines their musical philosophy.

Periodicals

Gavin Edwards. "Rapper, Hipster, Huckster, Preacherman, Lover Boy, Thug Angel, Country Aficionado, Wresting Fan, Global Visionary… Wyclef Is All These Things And More," *Rolling Stone*, October 12, 2000.

Melissa Ewey. "Wyclef's World." *Ebony*, May 1998.

Christopher John Farley. "Not Your Father's Hip-Hop." *Time*, February 12, 1996.

Greg Milner. "My Life in Music: Wyclef Jean." *Spin*, December 2003.

Gail Mitchell. "Sounds Without Borders: Wyclef Jean Melds Influences from Across the World." *Billboard*, November 24, 2007.

Lola Ogunnaike. "Clef Notes." *Vibe*, September 2000.

Deborah Sonta. "Wyclef Jean Confirms Plan to Run for Haitian Presidency. *Sarasota (FL) Herald Tribune*, August 5, 2010.

Internet Sources

Saxon Baird. "How Many Mics? Revisiting the Fugees' 'The Score' 15 Years Later." *Prefix*, October 27, 2011. www.prefixmag.com/features/the-fugees/fugees-the-score-review/57497.

Steven Baker and Julia Hoppock. "Nightline Playlist: Wyclef Jean," ABC News, December 8, 2007. www.abcnews.go.com/Nightline/story?id=3969239.

Audi Cornish. "Politics and Music in Wyclef Jean's Haitian Experience." Transcript of Radio Interview with Wyclef Jean. *All Things Considered.* NPR, November 27, 2010. www.npr.org/templates/transcript/transcript.php?storyId=131627159.

Joseph Guyler Delva. "Wyclef Jean Registers as Haiti Presidential Contender." Reuters, August 6, 2010. www.reuters.com/article/2010/08/06/us-haiti-wyclef-idUSTRE6745FD20100806.

Louise Gannon. "Wyclef Jean: He's Gone from Robbing a Store at Gunpoint to Global Superstar," *Mail Online* (London), November 10, 2007. www.dailymail.co.uk/home/moslive/article-491341/Wyclef-Jean-Hes-gone-robbing-store-gunpoint-global-superstar.html.

Genevieve Hassan. "Profile: Wyclef Jean." BBC, August 4, 2010. www.bbc.co.uk/news/entertainment-arts-10866989.

Wyclef Jean. "Inspiration All Around." *Huffington Post*, August 13, 2010. www.huffingtonpost.com/wyclef-jean/inspiration-all-around_b_681151.html.

Stephen Kurczy. "Wyclef Jean: Preacher's Son to Rap Star to Presidential Contender." *Christian Science Monitor*, August 6, 2010. www.csmonitor.com/World/Americas/2010/0806/Wyclef-Jean-Preacher-s-son-to-rap-star-to-presidential-contender.

Pete Lewis. "Wyclef Jean: Perfect Gentleman." *Blues & Soul*. www
.bluesandsoul.com/feature/360/wyclef_jean_perfect_gentleman.

Mariah Whittaker. "Wyclef Jean's Mission in Haiti." *Caribbean Belle* (Trinidad and Tobago). www.caribbeanbelle.com/interviews/wyclef-jean.php.

Websites

Fugees Official Site (www.thefugees.com). Official website of the Fugees that includes a newsletter sign-up, as well as links to each of its members' official sites, their music videos, and their official store.

Wyclef Jean President! (http://wyclefjeanpresident.com). A blog that has posted news updates about Wyclef Jean since 2001 and closely followed his presidential campaign in 2010.

Wyclef Jean's Blog (http://www.wyclef.com). The musician's official homepage and blog, featuring "Clef Notes" concert and tour dates, videos, and new music samples

Yéle Haiti (www.yele.org). The organization's official website contains news, videos, an online store, and information on various projects and programs as well as how to get involved.

Index

A

Acting
  Hill, Lauryn, 28
  Michel, Pras, 43
  Third Watch, 51
Adolescence
  crime, 8, 20–21
  Fugees, formation of, 25–26
  musical interests, 23–24
  romance, 27
Adoption, 57
Apollo Theater talent show, 24
Aristide, Jean-Bertrand, 74
Arrest, 63–64
Automobile accident, 21
Automobile collection, 59–60
Awards and honors
  Do Something Awards, 62–63
  Grand Officer of the National Order of Honor and Merit, 82, 83
  The Miseducation of Lauryn Hill, 42, 43
  The Score, 32, 33

B

Barrett, Syd, 46
Benefit concerts
  The Carnival, 61–62
  Clef's Kids, 63
  Port-au-Prince, 1997, 35, 36, 37, 38, 39
Bennett, Tony, 72
Berger, Ken, 70–71
Bieber, Justin, 72
Big Beat Records, 24
Black Entertainment Television, 54, 82
Black magic, 14–15
Blige, Mary J., 63
Block Party (documentary), 54
Bloomberg, Michael, 63–64
Blunted on Reality (album), 30–31
Bono, 59, 62, 62
Booga Basement, 27, 29, 31
Boute, Maarten, 67, 69
Brooklyn, New York, 16
Business, 57, 58

C

Car collection, 59–60
The Carnival (album), 41
The Carnival benefit concerts, 61–62
The Carnival II: Memoirs of an Immigrant (album), 56
Celebrities, 63
Celebrity Apprentice (television show), 59
Chappelle, Dave, 54
Charities
  The Carnival benefit concerts, 61–62
  Fugees, 35, 36
  goodwill ambassadorship, 73, 75, 82
  Haitian relief effort, 11, 12, 13
  "We Are the World" (song remake), 71–72, 72
  Yéle Foundation, 64–67, 66, 69
Charity Navigator, 70–71
Childhood
  crime, 20–21
  Haiti, 14–16
  move to New Jersey, 16–17
  music, 18–19
  punishments, 21, 23
Children, 57, 63
Christian rock, 18
Clapton, Eric, 66
Claudinette, Marie, 26, 27, 34, 40, 47, 57, 58
Clef's Kids, 63
Clinton, George, 62
Collaborations, 50, 52–53, 56
Columbia Records, 30–31
Concerts
  2012, 83, 84
  band tension, 37, 39
  benefit concerts, 38
  The Carnival benefit concerts, 61–62
  Clef's Kids, 63

Fugees, 35, 36
Fugees reunion, 54
Port-au-Prince, 1997, 35–36
Controversy
  lifestyle, 67
  presidential campaign, 77–78
  Yéle Foundation tax controversy, 69–71
Crime, 8, 20–21
Croix des Bouquets, 14–16

D
Damon, Matt, 66
Davis, Clive, 52, 52–53
Deforestation, 66–67
Destiny's Child, 61, 63
Do Something Awards, 62–63
Duplesis, Jerry, 31, 35, 41, 48, 69
Duvalier, François and Jean-Claude, 74

E
Earthquake, Haiti, 11, *12*, 68–71, 82
The Ecleftic: 2 Sides II a Book (album), 44–45, 47–48
Elliot, Missy, 50
Emergency relief. *See* Relief efforts
Exact Change (musical group), 23–24

F
Family
  adoption of daughter, 57
  grandparents, 14–15
  mother, *20*
  music, importance of, 18–19
  presidential campaign, 79
  See also Romance and marriage
Fashion, 57, *58*
Feel Good Music (album), 82–83
Fugees, 29
  Blunted on Reality (album), 30–31
  Booga Basement recording studio, 27, 29
  charities, 35, 36
  concerts, 35, 35–36
  discontent, 37, 39
  formation of, 25–26
  reunion, 54

The Score (album), 31–34
  solo efforts, 41–42
  success, 10, 34
  "Where Fugees At?", 45
"Fug-Gee-La" (Song), 34
Fusha Designs, 57, *58*

G
Gangsta rap, 32, 33–34
Gilmour, David, 46
Goodwill ambassadorship, 73, 75, 82
Grammy awards, *33*
  The Miseducation of Lauryn Hill, 42, 43
  The Score, 32
  Wyclef Presents . . . the Carnival, nominations for, 41
Grand Officer of the National Order of Honor and Merit, 82, *83*
Grandmaster Flash and the Furious Five, 22, *22*
Grandparents, 14–15
Guitar playing, 36

H
Haiti
  benefit concert, 35, 37, 39
  childhood, 14–16
  earthquake of 2010, 68–71, 75
  efforts to help, 10–11, *12*, 13
  goodwill ambassadorship, 73, 75, 82
  history, 17
  national pride, 39, *39*–40
  political corruption, 74
  presidential campaign, 75–80, *76*, *78*, 79–80
  relief efforts, 13
  Yéle Foundation, 64–67
Hill, Lauryn, 28, *42*
  affair with, 40
  attempt to reconcile with, 47
  benefit concert, 39
  biography, 28
  Fugees, formation of, 25–26
  The Miseducation of Lauryn Hill, 42, 43
Hip-hop
  Blunted on Reality, 30–31
  childhood, 18

father's dislike of, 23
Gangsta Rap, 32, 33–34
history, 22, *22*
The Score, 31–34
Honors. *See* Awards and honors
Hoodstock, 36
Hotel Rwanda (movie), 55, *55*
Houston, Whitney, 52–53, 63

I
"If I Was President" (song), 81
If I Was President (EP), 81–82

J
J Records, 52–53
Jackson, Michael, 71–72
Jay-Z, 63
Jazz, 23
Jean, Angelina Claudinette, 57
Jean, Gesner
　Clef's Kids concert, 63
　death of, 49–50, *50*
　hip-hop, dislike of, 23
　music, 18
　New Jersey, move to, 16–17
　punishments, 21
Jean, Samuel, 49, 76, 78
Johnson, Dwayne, 45
Jolie, Angelina, 65–66
Jones, Norah, 56, *57*
Jones, Quincy, 71–72
Joseph, Raymond, 73, 75, 76

K
Kennedy, Kerry, 76
Keyes, Alicia, 63
Knowles, Beyoncé, 61

L
LaBelle, Patti, 47, 50
Lifestyle, 11, 13, 34, 59–60, 67, 77–78
"Lift Every Voice and Sing" (song), 36, 63
L'ouverture, Toussaint, 17, *17*

M
Magic, 14–16
Marriage. *See* Romance and marriage

Martelly, Michel, 79, 80, 82, 83
Masquerade (album), 45–46
Michel, Prakazrel "Pras," 25–26, 39, 43, *43*, 47, 77
"A Million Voices" (song), 54–55
The Miseducation of Lauryn Hill (album), 42, 43
Movies, 28, 43, 51
Multiculturalism, 56
Music
　Big Beat Records, 24
　Booga Basement, 27, 29
　The Carnival II: Memoirs of an Immigrant, 56
　childhood, 18–19
　The Ecleftic: 2 Sides II a Book, 44–45
　Feel Good Music, 82–83
　Fugees' concerts, 35–36
　guitar, 36
　Haiti, 16
　hip-hop history, 22
　If I Was President (EP), 81–82
　The Preacher's Son (album), 50–53, 54–55
　Ruffhouse Records contract, 29–30
　The Score (album), 31–34
　styles, 8, 10, 23
　videos, 34
　Wyclef Presents . . . the Carnival, 41

N
National pride, *39*, 39–40
Natural disasters, 64–65, 68–71, 75, 82
NetAid, *62*, 62–63
"New Day" (song), 62
New Jersey, 16–17
New York City, 16, 63–64, *84*

O
O'Connor, Sinéad, 59
106 and Park (television show), 82
The Oprah Winfrey Show (television show), 70
"Out of the Jungle" (song), 24, *25*

P
Parents, 16–17, 18–19, *20*, 47–48
Penn, Sean, 77–78

Index **101**

Personality, 8, 26–27
Pink Floyd, 45
Politics, 10–11, 74–80, *76*, *78*, 79–80
Port-au-Prince benefit concert, 35, 36
Poverty, 14–15
The Preacher's Son (album), 50–53, 54–55
Presidential campaign, 75–80, *76*, *78*, 79–80
Préval, René, 74, 75
Protest, 63–64

R
Rap. *See* Gangsta rap; Hip-hop
"Ready or Not" (music video), 34
Recording studios, 24, 27, 29–30, 31
Refugee Camp, 36
Relief efforts, 11, 12, 13, 64–65, 71–72, *72*, 75
Religion
  music, 18–19
  personality, 8
  presidential campaign, 77
  voodoo, 14–15
Residency requirements for presidential candidates, 78–79
Richie, Lionel, 71–72
Rock and roll, 45, 46
Rolling Stone Do Something Award, 62–63
Romance and marriage, 26, 26–27, 40, 58
Ruffhouse Records, 29–30
Rwanda, 55–56

S
Santana, Carlos, 50, 52
The Score (album), 10, 31–34
Shooting, 79–80, *80*, 81
Siblings, 19, *19*
Simmons, Russell, 63
Simon, Paul, 56
Social activism
  "Out of the Jungle," 24
  The Preacher's Son (album), 54–55
  protest of teachers' pay cut, 63–64
  Rwanda, 55–56
  The Score, 33–34

Solo work
  The Ecleftic: 2 Sides II a Book, 44–45, 47–48
  Fugee bandmembers, 41–43
  genres, 10
  Masquerade, 45–46
  Wyclef Presents . . . the Carnival, 41
Songwriting, 50, 53, 54–55

T
Tax controversy, 69–71, 78
Teachers pay cuts, 63–64
Television
  acting, 51, *51*
  Celebrity Apprentice, 59
  106 and Park (television show), 82
  The Oprah Winfrey Show, 70
Theakston, Rob, 53
Third Watch (television show), 51, *51*
Timberland Company, 66, 67
Tranzlator Crew. *See* Fugees
Tropical Storm Jeanne, 64–67
Trump, Donald, 59

V
Videos, 34
Viv Ansamm Party, 75–76
"Vocab" (song), 30
Voodoo, 14–15

W
"We Are the World" (song remake), 71–72, *72*
Wealth, 11, 13, 77–78
Weingarten, Randi, 64
"Where Fugees At?" (song), 45
Wyclef Jean Foundation, 62
Wyclef Presents . . . the Carnival (album), 41

Y
Yéle Foundation, 11, *12*, 13, 64–69, *65*, *66*
Youth activism, 76–77

Picture Credits

Cover Photo: © CMF/ZJF WENN Photos/Newscom
© Allstar Picture Library/Alamy, 55
© Andrew Lichtenstein/Sygma/Corbis, 15, 38
© AP Images/Ariana Cubillos, 66
© AP Images/Daniel Morel, 35
© AP Images/Jennifer Graylock, 26
© AP Images/Paul Warner, 28
© AP Images/Ramon Espinosa, 80
© AP Images/Todd Plitt/PictureGroup, 67
© Ben Gabbe/Getty Images, 84
© Bettmann/Corbis, 17
© Corey Sipkin/NY Daily News Archive via Getty Images, 44
© David Corio/Redferns/Getty Images, 29
© Dennis Van Tine/Retna Ltd./Corbis, 12
© Djamilla Rosa Cochran/WireImage/Getty Images, 20
© Ebet Roberts/Redferns/Getty Images, 22
© Eric Liebowitz/Warner Bros./Getty Images, 51
© Ethan Miller/Getty Images, 9
© Frederic Dupoux/Getty Images, 76
© Gary Gerschoff/WireImage/Getty Images, 57
© Jean Jacques Augustin/EPA /Landov, 83
© Jeff Christensen/Reuters/Landov, 33
© Jeff Kravitz/FilmMagic/Getty Images, 42
© Joe Raedle/Getty Images, 78
© Kevin Mazur/WireImage/Getty Images, 72
© KMazur/WireImage/Getty Images, 62
© Kristy Leibowitz/Getty Images, 19
© L. Cohen/WireImage/Getty Images, 52
© Nicholas Kamm/AFP/Getty Images, 68
© Noel Vasquez/Getty Images, 43
© Randy Brooke/WireImage/Getty Images, 58
© Ricki Rosen/Corbis Saba, 74
© Roger Kisby/Getty Images, 65
© T. Hopkins/Corbis, 60
© Time & Life Pictures/Getty Images, 39

About the Author

Elizabeth Hoover is a writer based in Pittsburgh, where she writes about art, music, and books for a variety of publications.